TOLSTOY AT
YASNAYA POLYANA

Also by Patricia Chute

Eva's Music
Castine

TOLSTOY AT
YASNAYA POLYANA

HIS LIFE AND WORK IN THE CHARMED WORLD OF HIS ESTATE

PATRICIA CHUTE

Cornelia & Michael Bessie Books
An Imprint of HarperCollins*Publishers*

Photographs on pages 4, 9, 28, 42, and 47 from the estate of Wilbur Atwater. All others reproduced by permission of the L. N. Tolstoy Museum in Moscow.

FIRST EDITION

Designed by Cassandra J. Pappas

Library of Congress Cataloging-in-Publication Data

Chute, Patricia.
    Tolstoy at Yasnaya Polyana : his life and work in the charmed world of his estate / Patricia Chute.—1st ed.
        p.   cm.
    Includes index.
    ISBN 0-06-039131-6
    1. Tolstoy, Leo, graf, 1828–1910—Homes and haunts—Ĭάsnaiă Poliăna (Tul'skaiă oblast', R.S.F.S.R.) 2. Ĭάsnaiă Poliăna (Tul'skaiă oblast', R.S.F.S.R.)—Pictorial Works.   I. Title.
PG3401.C48   1991
89173'3—dc20   90-55924

---

91 92 93 94 95 AC/RRD 10 9 8 7 6 5 4 3 2 1

CONTENTS

ACKNOWLEDGMENTS

My gratitude to those who helped me with this book extends to two continents. In the Soviet Union, I owe thanks to Georgi Isachenko, director of V.A.A.P.; to Maksim Markovich, head of the Tolstoy State Museum in Moscow; and to Olga Yevgenyevna Yershova and Tatyana Konstaninovna Popovinka, assistant curators at the Tolstoy State Museum, who helped us select the historic pictures for this book. We were lucky to have the services of Robert Tateosevich Papikan, our exuberant photographer, who reshot the archival pictures that we chose, and in short order, too, so that I could take the negatives home with me four days later. And it is here, in Moscow, that I might best make note of the contribution of my husband, Dick Chute. As we ploughed through stack after stack of old Tolstoy photographs, I have a certain memory of him striding down the hall with boxes of pictures, making lists, keeping his head. It was fun.

At Yasnaya Polyana, on both visits, I was graciously received by a wonderful staff, most particularly by Galina Vasilyevna Alexeeva, scholar and curator. I am deeply grateful to our extraordinarily capable photographic research assistant and interpreter, Joanne Turnbull, who lives in Moscow. As she guided us past one hurdle after another, everything we did began to assume a kind of enchantment which was very much of her making.

In the United States, I should begin by acknowledging the person who lent me the first encouragement for this book, Henry Erhlich. Family friends take on many colorations; through the years, and to this day, Henry Erhlich grows in importance to us. My mother, Peggy Lamson, always an inspiration to me, interrupted work on her own book on many an afternoon to read passages of mine. My nephew, Whitman Knapp, offered invaluable editorial help. Abbott Gleason steadied my ship in the early days of this project. Friends lent books and encouragement (even a Russian language typewriter): William Crout, Deane Lord, Pearl and Dan Bell, Josephine Murray, Blair Clark, Hugh Truslow, Ann Herbert, Lois Bowen. Kitty Galbraith said she had an old trunk with a letter from her grandfather about a visit he made to Tolstoy at Yasnaya Polyana in 1897. Could she dig it out? Yes, she did.

I had the privilege of spending an afternoon in Florida with Tolstoy's granddaughter, Mme. Vera Tolstoy. She is a handsome woman with vivid memories. I was moved to hear Tolstoy referred to as "Grandfather."

Professor Robert Szulkin of Brandeis University proved a gentle guide and a generous friend. His book-lined office grew to feel like an old Russian posting station, a place to take orientation and reassurance. It is to him that these final thanks are offered.

PREFACE

Unlike the grave sites of other Russian heroes, Leo Tolstoy's place of burial is very simple. In a clearing in the forest at Yasnaya Polyana, the estate where he was born, one finds a raised rectangle of earth, surrounded by trees and brush. I was surprised at the size of the site; it is small, and the grave itself is unmarked—no statues, no epitaphs carved in stone. As a boy, Leo Tolstoy played on this very spot with his three older brothers; here they pursued their favorite games, the Ant Brotherhood and the Secret of the Green Stick. It is easy to imagine little boys sliding down nearby ravines, dodging each other through the trees. The presence of the grave does not interrupt this imagery.

Not a quarter of a mile away, down a rutted road, is the place where Tolstoy's life began. He was born in 1828, on the second floor of the main house of the estate. It is unusual to find the locus of life's beginning and end at such very close proximity. For Tolstoy, the journey in between was monumental.

He was born in an extraordinary time, one over which he was to exert huge influence. The landowning gentry of prerevolutionary Russia enjoyed vast privilege, which was to erode by the end of his life. The monarchy, securely entrenched at the beginning of his life, was overturned by 1917, seven years after his death.

Nineteenth-century Russia saw an explosion of literary achievement. Pushkin's lyric verses formed the basis for a new literary language. Ivan Turgenev wrote delicately balanced works about conflicts between generations. Dostoyevsky's novels depicted men's darkest struggles, and Chekhov's plays found the perfect melancholy of the times.

But one voice seemed to dominate nineteenth-century Russia. With the publication in 1865 of *War and Peace,* Leo Tolstoy changed the landscape of modern literature. So prolific was he that his writings, novels, short stories, essays, and plays came to ninety volumes in all. He was a restless thinker; in his quest for truth he framed the moral questions that were then, and remain now, of singular importance. By what he stood for, as well as the timelessness of his fiction, Tolstoy transcended the boundaries of literary achievement. He was felt by many to be more powerful than the tsar.

In this century preceding the Bolshevik Revolution, life at court, the court of the Romanov tsars, glittered with opulence and splendor. An argumentative intelligentsia had gathered in St. Petersburg, the center of Russian liberalism. Among the gentry, the influence of the French Enlightenment was felt in all aspects of life: good wines, the temptations of republicanism and individual freedom, a lust for stylistic Europe. At home, upper-class parents spoke to their children in French.

Yet, in terms of numbers and social structure, nineteenth-century Russia remained unmistakably a land of peasants. A census taken in 1796 reveals that 95 percent of the population lived in the countryside, and a large majority of that number were *owned*—indentured serfs.

By 1847, 330 of them were owned by Leo Tolstoy. Contrary to English custom, where one is lucky to be born first, Russian tradition dictates that the youngest son inherit the family ancestral property. In April of 1847, at the age of nineteen, young Tolstoy became the master of Yasnaya Polyana; it was the birthplace of his mother and the scene of his own childhood. The legacy included two thousand acres of farmland and forest, a splendid two-story house, twenty outbuildings and a large stable, four ponds, and peasant villages containing 330 "souls," as they were then called.

Yasnaya Polyana was a place of remote and exquisite beauty, and it still is. Meticulously restored to the comfortable state in which it was left at the time of Tolstoy's death in 1910, the estate is presently open to the public, crowded with visitors, and considered a national shrine. Yet it feels utterly removed from daily, larger Russian experience. The nearby industrial city of

Tula, some few minutes away from the estate, seems distinctly another world.

Loosely translated, Yasnaya Polyana means "clear meadow" or "clear glade," but to say it out loud, Yas Na Ya, rhythmic and lulling, is to begin to understand the gentle sense of it as a cocoon, as a place which offered protection, guarded innocence, and a world of childhood games which created Tolstoy's moral framework. What one sees at Yasnaya Polyana today is a rather delicate, two-story European house with Russian trappings. The samovar is still on the dining room table. The house is built for an aristocrat, with room enough for two pianos, and yet there is an intimacy, a kind of sweetness, which suggests family life above formality. Standing in the first floor hall, with its bookcases and plain wood floors, one has the feeling that Tolstoy is about to come down the stairs. And the surrounding land, over which he walked and rode and planted—and agonized—as a kind of rugged perfection; its undulating fields and orchards are not spruced up, made orderly for tourists. Nature untrammeled. Tolstoy would have insisted on this.

In 1847 the property was in disarray, but then again, one might suggest, so was its new master. Tolstoy had withdrawn from the University of Kazan with a bad case of venereal disease, he was uncertain of his talents and his future, and he considered himself homely. A young man of vast intelligence, many contradictions, and no small vanity, his almost kinetic thinking carried him everywhere—to the philosophy of Rousseau, which enchanted him, to his sexual appetite, which disgusted him, to the state of his soul, which deeply concerned him. From his earliest years, Leo Tolstoy was possessed of an enlarged consciousness, an almost unbearable self-awareness, and an unerring eye for detail, not only of his own feelings but of all of life around him.

There was little in Tolstoy's early years to hint at the magnitude of what he was to become. As a young man he gained some fame with his early works—*The Raid, Childhood, The Cossacks*—but in 1865, the world was hardly prepared for *War and Peace*. It ran in installments in the journal *Russkii Vestnik* (*"Russian Herald"*) with various titles, to a length of over fourteen hundred pages, and soon was to transfix two continents. This extraordinary idyll, tracing the interwoven lives of three aristocratic families throughout the War of 1812, harnessed a nation's patriotism. Many of the characters and settings were taken from Tolstoy's own family life at Yasnaya Polyana.

In 1875, after the almost equal success of *Anna Karenina* (a novel he claimed to dislike), Tolstoy, in the public eye, took on some of the hugeness of Russia itself. In the grandeur of his work he was compared to Homer (a comparison he did not discourage), was often called the greatest master of literature of the nineteenth century, and was even described as being of towering physical proportions, although he was a man of average stature.

In his later years, after the torment of his spiritual crisis, with his long white beard and piercing eyes, Tolstoy looked like an Old Testament prophet. Compelling. Messianic. Anguished. As pilgrims and would-be disciples came to sit at his feet at Yasnaya Polyana, he became something akin to a living icon.

The world of Yasnaya Polyana, where his vision and memories were lodged, was certainly the principal formative influence of his life. The idyllic childhood and early moral preoccupations, as well as Tolstoy's identification with the plight of the peasants, his own viscerally felt bond with the working of the land, and his final flight—all took place at Yasnaya Polyana. The history of Russia can be felt in microcosm at Yasnaya Polyana; its passages through time—from the grand style of Tolstoy's grandfather, Count Volkonsky, to the freeing of the serfs, to the end of manorial life—were those of the nation.

The relationship between Leo Tolstoy and Yasnaya Polyana was complex, passionate—and instructive. In a man of many contradictions, Yasnaya Polyana provided him with a big one—how could he be the master of the estate and still condemn all ownership of property? What is justice? he asked. How shall man live?

Yet, in its splendid isolation, the estate provided Tolstoy with psychological distance (and a strategic retreat) from the practical concerns of reform and the anxiety of the literati, in a time of great change. He was left free, both by logistics and by temperament, to examine the large questions. From Yasnaya Polyana, he then launched his powerful attacks on the church, government, all institutions—as a member of the ruling class. And his moral authority was such that the tsars, four in his lifetime, dared not stop him. Others who, like he, were considered anarchists, such as Dostoyevsky, were sent into exile in Siberia. Tolstoy remained more or less untouched at Yasnaya Polyana.

The apple orchard, the peasants and their huts, the supremacy of nature—it was through this prism that he saw Russia; and it is through the same prism, in this book, that we will see him. To know him better, in his complexity and grandeur, we must know the place which provided his root system. How he was bound to Yasnaya Polyana and how it formed him, affected his writing, and, in the end, disenchanted him, is the subject of these next pages.

"I cannot imagine Russia, or my relationship to her, without my Yasnaya Polyana," he wrote. Having been there, having read him, neither can I.

AUTHOR'S NOTE: Throughout this book I will refer to Tolstoy by his English name, Leo, for it is by this name that he is known outside of Russia. Where appropriate (particularly in the chapters about his childhood), he will be referred to by his Russian name, Lev or Lev Nikolayevich.

Sonya's Russian name is Sofya Andreyevna, but he called her Sonya, and so will I.

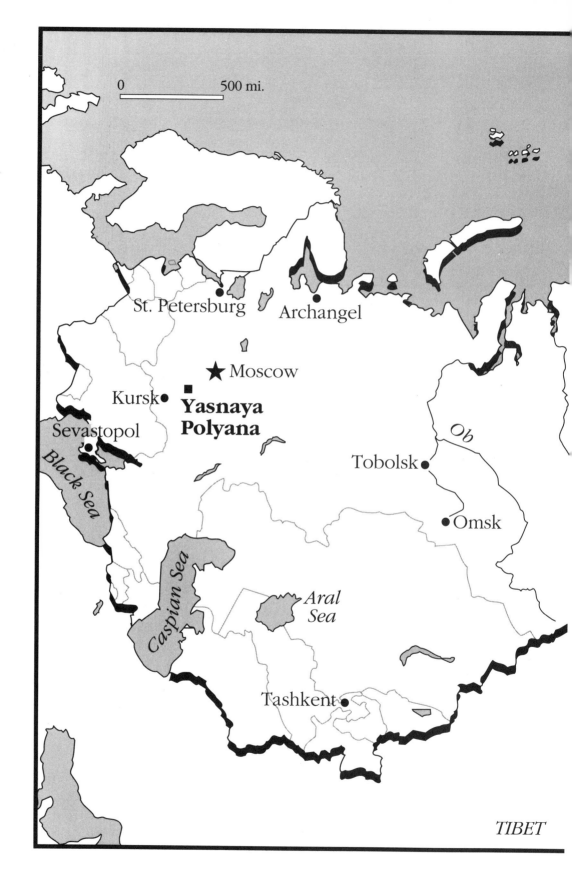

St. Petersburg

Archangel

★ Moscow

Kursk ■ **Yasnaya Polyana**

Sevastopol

Black Sea

Caspian Sea

Aral Sea

Tobolsk

Ob

Omsk

Tashkent

TIBET

0   500 mi.

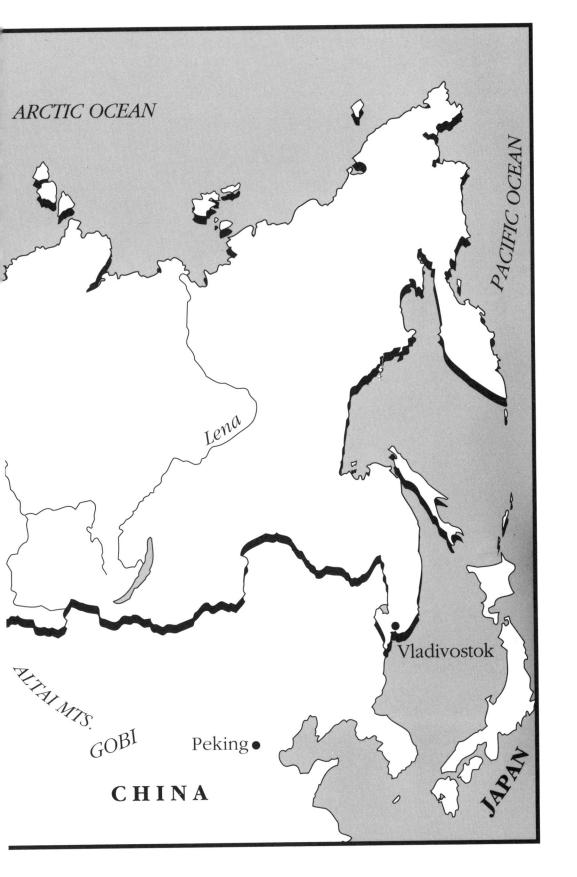

1

A SPLENDID ORPHAN AND THE GOLDEN AGE OF YASNAYA POLYANA [1828–1852]

For the occasion of his marriage Lev Nikolayevich Tolstoy bought a new carriage, known as a dormeuse; it was a sleeping coach, to be drawn by six horses and driven by a liveried coachman. Just hours after his wedding, at the Church of the Nativity, in the Kremlin, on the evening of September 23, 1862, Tolstoy assisted his young bride, Sofya Andreyevna Behrs, into the dormeuse; they were headed for his estate, Yasnaya Polyana, some 130 miles south.

The wedding had been festive, but now their departure was shrouded in gloom. The leave-taking ceremony, a Russian tradition of prayer and contemplation before departure, found a solemn and apprehensive wedding party. Although the Behrs family agreed that the marriage of their daughter to the thirty-four-year-old Count Tolstoy was a favorable one, Sonya was only eighteen, the courtship had been brief, and her family felt that she was being torn away from them. Her mother and sisters sobbed, Sonya sobbed, Tolstoy stood awkwardly nearby, and it was raining. When at last the carriage pulled away from the house, Sonya's mother uttered a cry which pierced the night; Sonya recorded in her diary that she would never forget it. A cry deep from a mother's heart. Tolstoy shifted in his seat.

In this lugubrious mood, the newlyweds rode out of Moscow into the night. The autumn rain brought a chill, the roads were rough. They did not know each other well. Spirits were raised slightly when they pulled in for the night at Biryulevo, where the local innkeeper, recognizing the Tolstoy name, offered them the suite reserved for the tsar. A samovar was brought out, tea was served. They managed to get through the wedding night, or so his diary records, but Tolstoy does make note of "her terror." The next evening the exhausted couple arrived at the gates of Yasnaya Polyana. At the main house, Tolstoy's beloved Aunt Toinette came forward to greet them, clutching an icon of the Mother of God. Tolstoy's brother Sergei waited beyond the doorway, holding the traditional tray of bread and salt—the emblem of hospitality.

Lev Nikolayevich and Sofya Andreyevna kissed the icon, crossed themselves, and embraced Aunt Toinette. Their life together at Yasnaya Polyana had begun.

He owned everything as far as the eye could see, or so it must have seemed to his bride. Leo Tolstoy was born into the seigneurial class of landowner (nobility with sure connections at court). He had been in full possession of the

Tolstoy at the age of twenty, just at about the time he became master of Yasnaya Polyana.

estate since the age of nineteen; it was, in some real sense, his own kingdom. He owned the serfs, approximately two thousand acres of land, forests, ponds, stables—even the village at the edge of the property. Tolstoy was born at Yasnaya Polyana, and it was here that he spent his boyhood, in a state of innocence and privilege. His autobiographical novel, *Childhood,* published ten years before his marriage, cherishes the immense familiarity of every corner of the estate, hallowed ground containing memories and myths, viscerally felt. Fortunately, Sonya had read it.

Although she had spent time in the country, Sonya Behrs was a child of the city. For the most part, her pleasures as a young girl had been devoted to reading, sewing, and rearranging the possessions in her room. The morning after her arrival from Moscow, the peasant women of the village, in keeping with local ritual, presented the baffled bride with a flapping hen decorated with ribbons, which she was expected to hold while the women chanted their lengthy welcoming songs.

Until the moment of his marriage, Tolstoy, preoccupied with his writing and bouts of travel, had been a somewhat lapsed master, and the condition of the estate at the moment of her arrival would have represented a challenge to anyone, much less an untutored city girl. The house, a long, two-story stone structure, was what remained of the more lavish, Italian-designed estate of Tolstoy's grandfather, Count Volkonsky. Volkonsky inherited the estate, known for its abundance of ash trees, and it was he who organized the building of the main house and laid out plans for the parks and gardens. Most gentry of any consequence in the eighteenth century had their houses designed by Europeans, as the effect of the Enlightenment swept through the Russian upper classes. Count Volkonsky was a precise man; a fleet of serfs tended minutely to both the master and his estate. Two sentries, in full dress, stood guard at the gateposts, almost as if in a play designed for an audience. Such was the feel of many eighteenth-century estates.

However, Lev Nikolayevich Tolstoy was of the informal school of landowner, who liked (for a time) to take care of his pigs himself, and the tenue of the place had fallen off a bit. The gardens were overrun, the interior of the house was decidedly spare, with whitewashed walls and bare floors. Despite its graceful windows overlooking the meadow, the second floor parlor was dimly lit and gloomy. Rough furniture made by the serfs. No carpets. Simple tallow candles. Fortunately, the walls of the main house were a foot and a half thick—essential for the oncoming winter.

The household staff, a pageant of figures from the feudal past, unkempt and thoroughly informal, roamed in and about the house in a kind of daze. The cook, Nikolai Mikhailovich, a leftover clarinet player from Grandfather Volkonsky's serf orchestra, was often too drunk to perform his duties, but, as Tolstoy was "terribly fond of drunks," all was excused. Agatha Mikhailovna, the housekeeper, another favorite from the past, kept cockroaches for pets. She was the guardian of the dogs of the estate, and most of them slept in her darkened room. In her youth she had served Tolstoy's grandmother. Once quite handsome, her appearance had now gone to eccentricity. Everyone called her Gasha. In her room, candles set next to the icon picturing St. Nicholas burned constant through the wild odor given off by the dogs. She also liked mice. For the most part, the house serfs slept anywhere they felt like, in the hall or the kitchen, wrapped in old blankets.

If the mise-en-scène at the house seemed daunting, the beauty of the property, the surrounding park, and dense forests did catch Sonya's fancy. From the gate house, the main road (the *prospekt*) leading up to the house was long and lovely, a wide path with pale sun filtering through the leaves of tall birches. Yasnaya Polyana is set in the heart of Tula Province, which possessed particularly fertile soil, and Sonya found herself surrounded by acres of well-

Peasant village in winter.

tilled, rolling farmland. Flocks of sheep dotted the property. How could she help but be charmed by the ponds—yes, they could ice-skate there in the winter. Four clear ponds, surrounded with birches, now stocked for fishing. In her walks Sonya roamed the apple orchard and followed Lev Nikolayevich through the upper park, where he scrupulously tended his favorite plantings of pungent lime trees. Among the outbuildings, the graceful one-and-a-half-story wooden building where old Prince Volkonsky had lived briefly now housed a spinning room for the women serfs. Nearby sat an immense structure which served as the stables. Dogs roamed everywhere. Peasants' thatched huts, all part of the estate, were clustered, like satellites, in the fields and at the edge of the woodlands. From the top of the hill Sonya could see wanderers passing on the Old Kiev Road, making their way in carts or on foot, often stopping at Yasnaya to rest. And she saw the serfs working in the fields.

Like most Russians, Sonya did not question the presence of indentured serfs; it was simply the natural order of things. It was Peter the Great's repressive measures that worsened the lot of the peasants, and Catherine the Great, the Prussian who ruled Russia from 1762 to 1796, is credited with nailing down the structure of serfdom. Once free and living in poverty in communal settings, by the nineteenth century most peasants were owned. By 1847, Leo Tolstoy's peasants, inhabiting rudimentary huts and sleeping on their stoves, were housed in farming villages near the manor house. Their numbers included the fourteen or fifteen house serfs, many of whom felt a proprietary bond to the house which had passed down through generations of their own families. Sonya was their new mistress. To her credit, she held onto the squawking chicken on that early September morning.

Nestled in among ash groves and forests, the world of Yasnaya Polyana offered its own version of the golden age. The estate was designed for self-sufficiency. Sonya entered a world which was self-contained, circular—its own reason for being. And isolated. So very isolated. Country estates in Russia were, for the most part, autonomous little enclaves, built around an apathetic peasantry and, often, a surprisingly independent-thinking gentry. The seat of the monarchy seemed far away, and social insularity and distance gave the estate owner the opportunity to create his own rules; therefore, quite frequently, benevolence and independent thinking did flourish in the hands of certain landowners. Constructed around acceptance and simplicity, folklore and the comfort of the gentry, the country estate did as much to keep Russia fragmented as any social force could.

The farmland was planned for both sustenance and profit. Pigs bought for breeding mostly ended up on the table. Cabbage was grown for sale, for money to buy the few necessary pieces of equipment, such as fencing and rope. The economy of the estate was that of an independent nation. Cloth was woven in-house, clothes fashioned in the weaving room. Serfs crafted the furniture and cobbled their shoes. Mushrooms and berries for jams were abundant. Leo Tolstoy fancied himself a beekeeper, and for a time there was a seasonal yield of honey. Yasnaya Polyana in the nineteenth century still very much adhered to its original eighteenth-century design—patriarchal, antiprogress, insular, cut off from vulgar influences. Austere in places, but a kingdom of its own. And the door was always open; guests were received with excitement and a certain amount of pageantry. The Russian tradition of elaborate, wildly fulsome hospitality speaks of both the warmth of the Slavic heart and the distance and isolation of the manor houses.

The history of the estate bore with it a colorful panorama of aristocratic figures. Although Tolstoy's family could be traced back to their fourteenth-century ancestor, the nobleman Indris, they had been very much a part of the ruling class since the time of the first Romanov tsar, in 1613. Yasnaya Polyana was given its grandeur by Leo Tolstoy's maternal grandfather, Count Volkonsky, who inherited the place from his father. Volkonsky had served the court of Catherine the Great as ambassador to Berlin. When he felt the fleeting disfavor (possibly imagined) of her son, Mad Emperor Paul, Count Volkonsky simply retired to his own kingdom at Yasnaya Polyana to devote himself to its management and to the upbringing of his only child, Princess Marya.

At that time, around 1800, the main house was elaborate, an imposing central structure with tall columns and balconies, flanked by two wings. Total number of rooms: thirty-two. Old Count Volkonsky was of the feared-but-loved school of landholding gentry—meticulous, stern, formal, and requiring a bit of pampering: Every morning a small serf orchestra played the music of Haydn under his window to ease his passage into the day. Count Volkonsky is pictured vividly, if not exactly, in *War and Peace*—Count Bolkonsky, who ruled Bald Hills. Most of Count Volkonsky's energy was spent teaching languages and mathematics to his pliant, homely, but kindly daughter, Marya.

Unfortunately, no portrait remains of Princess Marya, Leo Tolstoy's mother. She died when he was two, and he could only claim unconscious memories of her. But they were warm and worshipful, these memories, and the fact that she died before he could know her is a most significant fact in Tolstoy's life.

"In my conception of her there is only her spiritual figure," he wrote, "and all that I know about her is beautiful."[1] The man who idealizes his mother is not new to the annals of psychology, but in Tolstoy's case his elevated feelings for her stayed with him all of his life. Two years before his own death, he would record in his diary: ". . . I walk in the garden and I think of my mother, of maman; I do not remember her, but she has always been an ideal of saintliness for me."[2]

Although by all reports Princess Marya was not pretty, she possessed a keen, well-developed intelligence and gentleness of spirit. Her marriage to Count Nicholas Tolstoy was arranged by their families, and in some haste, as she was thirty-one years old, an age considered past the prime for betrothal in Russian society.

Tolstoy's father, Count Nicholas, was a blue blood—but dead broke. Princess Marya was heiress to a fortune. On such foundations many reason-

Portrait of Tolstoy's father, Count Nikolai Ilyich Tolstoy.

able marriages existed, and from all reports, theirs was a respectful, perhaps even happy, one. Five children were born in eight years. Four boys—Nikolai, Dmitri, Sergei, and Lev—and a girl, Marya. The exact cause of the death of Princess Marya Tolstoy is vague—as was the practice of medicine at that time—but biographers suggest that the exhaustion of constant childbearing might have caused her declining health. But in her person, in her memory, rested all of the vestiges of the ideal Russian woman. Serene, maternal, pure of spirit—for Lev Nikolayevich his mother's image was so hallowed, her nature so keenly felt, that she seemed to inhabit the walls.

From everything we can discover, Tolstoy was an unusually sensitive child. Minutely tended to by his nurse, housed in an upstairs nursery with his sister, his imagination and consciousness developed early and vividly. He felt everything intensely—nature, the bran in his bathwater, the odor given off by his Aunt Aline. Apprehensive at first, when finally allowed to move freely throughout the house he tended to cling to the hand of his tutor, sensing danger in stationary objects, bursting into tears often, so much so that he was nicknamed Lev Crybaby (Lyova Ryova) by his older brothers.

And yet, several months later, when he wished to understand what it would be like to fly away and leave the earth, in an impulsive moment little Lev simply jumped out of a third-floor window. He knocked himself out. Fortunately, the cook was nearby, and the flyer was unharmed. An attempt, he admitted, "to impress the others."

After his morning lessons Lev and his brothers were left free to roam through the fields (their tutor, Fodor Ivanovich Rossel, nearby), to swim in the Voronka River, to play in the forests, or, should one of his aunts wish an outing, to ride in the cabriolet (an open carriage with springs) for a visit to a neighboring village. In the winter everyone accepted the isolation brought on by the snow and drifts—the Dutch stoves provided enough warmth, and card games and music filled slow-moving evenings.

As Yasnaya Polyana remained a patriarchal establishment, life centered largely around the schedule of the children's father, who liked to hunt. Dinner was a highly formal affair. Everyone waited in relative silence for Count Tolstoy, who, at an exact moment, appeared from his study and ushered his mother, Countess Pelageya, to her seat. At that point conversation could, and did, begin, as a fleet of servants in frock coats and white gloves ladled out the soup. They remained in constant attendance through dessert, one servant standing behind each chair. An ancient retainer named Tikhon waited pa-

Peasant girls with water buckets.

tiently nearby until the meal was over, that he might give the master his favorite pipe. In this golden age an aspect of theater could be felt, especially at mealtime.

When Lev Nikolayevich was nine his father, on an errand in the nearby city of Tula, dropped dead on the street. The circumstances were never fully understood; there was a suggestion that he had been robbed by two of his own serfs. Yasnaya Polyana was plunged into mourning. The five children of this most practical union of Marya Volkonsky and Nicholas Tolstoy thus became orphans. Unlike his mother, who remained something of a vision, Lev Nikolayevich did know his father, who was handsome and affectionate. His sudden death was terrifying. Death, a specter which was to both haunt and beguile Tolstoy all of his life, had struck twice. Yet a short time later, a tiny hint of detachment, a detachment which was later to serve Tolstoy the writer, could be detected, as young Lev noted that he was the center of a different kind of attention and that his status of the "complete orphan" interested him. In his autobiographical novel *Childhood,* which is a kind of synthesis of fiction and nonfiction, he describes it this way: "Before and after the funeral I did not cease crying and felt sad, but I am ashamed to remember that sadness, for it was always mingled with some selfish feeling; now a desire to show that I grieved more than anyone else. Besides this I felt a kind of enjoyment at knowing myself to be unhappy, and tried to stimulate my consciousness of unhappiness, and this egotistical feeling, more than anything else, stifled real sorrow in me."[3] His heightened awareness, the ability to be conscious of the self and to be outside of the self, had begun to gather force.

At Count Tolstoy's death the children were left in the care of two aunts. At the helm, briefly, sat the deeply religious and somewhat batty Countess Aline, who, when she was not busy praying, entertained a slew of beggars and simple-minded truth seekers. Young Lev developed an early appreciation for these holy fools of the time, who wandered into the house constantly from the nearby Old Kiev Road.

Far more significant to Lev was the love of his delicate, enchanting Aunt Toinette, who was to devote her life to the care of the Tolstoy children. She was gentle, warm, and self-sacrificing. "I never thought of her as being pretty or not pretty," he later recorded. "I simply loved her—loved her eyes, her smile, and her dusky broad little hand with its energetic little cross vein."[4] Tolstoy's grandmother, Countess Pelageya, an authoritative creature, attempted, in the short time before her own death, to be a soothing force.

But apart from the uneven influence of these well-intentioned women, the void left by the death of two parents was filled by Yasnaya Polyana itself. The estate, with memories incased in every corner, every path, the immense familiarity of the servants, the steady passage of the Christmas rituals and name day festivals—the property itself, in its changelessness, served as a kind of emblem for the missing parents. The seasonal routines, idyllic, secure days, the preeminence of the patterns of nature, allowed the developmental needs of Lev Nikolayevich to become rooted in the place itself. Instead of his mother and father, he had his Aunt Toinette—and Yasnaya, its woods, the river, and, as he described it, "the gentle caress of the old house."

Everyone kept busy and went to church on the holidays and accepted life. Uncomplicated, unhurried days. Tutors, willing serfs, sleighs, picnics—and plenty of time to think. Tolstoy remembers riding out in the yellow cabriolet with his grandmother to the hazelnut trees, and there, having the servants, Petrusha and Matyusha, "pull down to her branches with clusters of ripe nuts, and she gathered them into the bag."

In the world of branch-lowering servants there also has to be a blind storyteller, and Grandmother Pelageya had him. Lyov Stepanovich was his name, and he wore a blue frock coat with white puffs on the sleeves. "He was brought in merely for the purpose of narrating stories," Tolstoy recalls. "He lived somewhere in the house, and during the whole day he was not seen, but in the evening he came up into my grandmother's bedroom . . . I remember only the moment when the candle was put out and there remained only a little light in front of the gilded icons, and my grandmother, in white, lay high on the cushions and from the window was heard the even, quiet voice of Lyov Stepanovich. 'A certain powerful king had only one son . . .' "[5]

With his brothers he learned to swim in the Voronka River, which curled through the property. They all learned to ride and to hunt, and at teatime there were plenty of pastries, *vatrushki,* and strawberry jam. Lev was close to his brothers. "With Nicolenka [Nikolai] I wished to associate, to talk, Sery-

The four Tolstoy brothers, photographed about 1852. Left to right: *Sergei, Nikolai, Dmitri, and Lev.*

ozha [Sergei] I only wished to imitate. He took to keeping his own hens and chickens. I did the same."[6] Yasnaya Polyana seemed designed to perpetuate innocence and the simplicity of human experience.

But there was one hideous, unwelcome visitor: The terror of death lurked in the background, etched on Tolstoy's consciousness. Maman. Papa. His grandmother. The inescapable reality of death—he felt it constantly. The reality of death—Was it that which caused such a heightened feeling for the joys of childhood?

"Happy, happy irrecoverable time of childhood!" Tolstoy wrote in *Childhood*. "How can one not love and cherish its memory?" Irrecoverable perhaps, but as a man Tolstoy did, in fact, in a very real sense, seek to recover the idyllic aspects of life, the possibility of virtue and purity, which were at the core of the world of Yasnaya Polyana. Why should not earthly happiness belong to everybody?

The pivotal impressions on Tolstoy's early years must of course have included the deaths of his parents and the gentle authority of Aunt Toinette, but it was a childhood game that grew to become one of the principal forces to shape his life. The Tolstoy children created their own little club and named it the Ant Brotherhood. The tale that they wove into its midst was called the Secret of the Green Stick. The Secret of the Green Stick sounds like something one might find in a contemporary bookstore, a quickly forgotten children's who-done-it. Yet the Tolstoy children's innocent fantasy grew to be a grown man's point of departure for an entire way of life.

Huddled under chairs in the dining room, the children made up their own version of attainable paradise: In this special world there would be an end to all disease and unhappiness. Only universal love and well-being would exist. As Nikolai, the creator of the game, wove the tale, the secret to achieving this continuous happiness could not be revealed but was written on a green stick. The green stick was buried in a spot where they often played, a ravine near the main house.

No biographer has missed the significance of little Lev Nikolayevich and his brothers creating their own idealized society; but in the absence of parents, the game, begun as the five Tolstoy children romped in the forest and built their secret world, proved to have some of the wished-for moral axioms that parents often impart to children. Put an end to quarreling. Let love flower in every heart. Nikolai was ten, Sergei was eight, Dmitri six, and impressionable little Lev just five when the boys declared their yearning for a life free from suffering. The Secret of the Green Stick may have a simplistic air, but its implications for Lev Nikolayevich were to become permanent. Why not a perfect world? Why not look for the One Truth?

Some sixty years later, as he searched for a new moral order, he wrote, "The ideal of the Ant Brothers, lovingly clinging to one another, though not under two armchairs curtained by handkerchiefs, but of all mankind under the wide dome of heaven, has remained the same for me. As I then believed that there existed a little green stick whereon was written the message which could destroy all evil in men and give them universal welfare, so I now believe that such truth exists and will be revealed to men, and will give them all its promises."[7]

It was this early ability to visualize a world free from evil and suffering, a world of earthly goodness, that stood at the foundation of Tolstoy's thinking. If some people, through the rough passage of time, choose to give up their first beliefs and early innocence, he certainly did not. As to the hallowed ground, the ravine at Yasnaya Polyana—"Since I must be buried somewhere," he wrote, "I have asked to be buried there." The secret of the green stick, never revealed, is buried with him.

As the splendid orphan reached thirteen, it was decided that he and his brothers should move to Kazan for the winters, with yet again another aunt, Pelageya Yushkov, so that they could attend the local university. They would come back to Yasnaya Polyana for holidays and summers. At this point Leo Tolstoy's precociousness began to be visible for all to see. It was the beginning of what might be described as his enlarged vision.

The unconscious preparation was all there. From his earliest days, when most boys were quite content to play in the mud, little Lev appeared to have developed for himself a kind of understanding of where he stood in the universe. "My definite reminiscences commence from the time when I was transferred downstairs to Fodor Ivanovich [his tutor] and my elder brothers," he recalled to Pavel Birukoff years later. "I experienced for the first time, and therefore more powerfully than ever, that feeling which is called the feeling of duty—the feeling of the Cross, which every man is called to bear."[8] It might be hard to believe this "feeling of the Cross" in a child of five or six, but then again the inner experience of Leo Tolstoy simply was never usual. And never would be. His early ability to develop conclusions, his own conclusions, to come by his own rational processes, propelled him forward.

Early in puberty, he read Pushkin's verses and Russian legends. Never much of a regular student, he often pored through novels and parts of the Bible until he was delirious. By the time he was thirteen he had read the works of Sterne and Rousseau, the Scriptures, the Lives of the Saints, and delved into their essential truths with a passion that astounded those around him. By fourteen, he no longer accepted the religious beliefs and conventions that he had been taught in early childhood. The world of Yasnaya Polyana was one in which Tolstoy developed a religious temperament, but his need to question, to push relentlessly toward newer truths, caused him to incorporate a different creed, uncertain in its particulars but clearly *his*. Perfecting oneself, he called it.

Moral perfection, physical perfection—perfection (he confessed in *A Confession*) in the eyes of others. And he was able to write, later, in *Boyhood*, "I often imagined myself a great man, discovering new truths for the benefit of mankind, and regarded the rest of humanity with proud consciousness of my own worth. But strangely enough when I encountered these other mortals, I felt shy of each of them . . ."[9] He read all of Pushkin, he read about the Napoleonic Wars, and he recorded both his thoughts and all of his sins (real or imagined) meticulously in a well-worn notebook. Most of all—"I remember that I was continually preoccupied with myself." To be sure, an enormous ego was building.

No account of the aristocracy is complete without the character of the mean-spirited tutor, and in Leo Tolstoy's life such a tutor really did exist. Prosper de St. Thomas was a young Frenchman, sharp, punitive, arrogant. He had been successful in terrifying young Leo with the threat of a beating, called him a "good-for-nothing," once locked him in a closet. But even Prosper de St. Thomas had to agree, "The boy has a head. He's a young Molière."[10]

Young Molière, in this case, had the misfortune to believe that he was homely. After a bout of wild horseback riding or exhausting reading, he would stand before the mirror and try to flatten down his hair, or even, in one miserable moment, cut off his eyebrows. His eyes were small and his nose wide. No, he was not as handsome as his brother Sergei. "The most vulgar, coarse and ugly features, little gray eyes that look more stupid than clever," he confided in the autobiographical *Youth*. "My face was that of a common muzhik, and so were my big hands and feet." From the University of Kazan, where he was stuck at the vulnerable age of fifteen, he redoubled his efforts to cast himself as a *man of distinction*. He would speak perfect French, he decided, have clean fingernails, learn to dance, and, above all, ". . . appear indifferent, to wear a certain air of distinguished and disdainful boredom at all times."

One can't help but cringe at the depth of his youthful anguish and the awkwardness of his resolution. Although Tolstoy was very much a part of the nobility, many of whom personified boredom because of their own limitations, this young nobleman was not capable of boredom. Life was too compelling, too stimulating, too full of contradictions. Instinctively, from his earliest years, Tolstoy had the ability to identify deeply with others. When the stable boy was beaten, Tolstoy wept. As half-mad pilgrims wandered into the house to rest (and to eat) he watched closely, he entered into their prayers, listened to their stories, with his heart open. Some thirty-five years later, as Tolstoy the writer brought the world *Anna Karenina,* the question was asked: How could he construct the complex character of Anna, he, a man, how could he understand her inner life? From an early and extraordinary awareness of others, their complexities became his, a super consciousness was at work to join him with nature, with the people around him, with the most delicate sounds, the smallest voice.

In its near-feudal isolation, the world of Yasnaya Polyana managed to remain rich and varied. On some estates enjoying the same isolation, people often just went crazy, as Gogol made vivid in *Dead Souls.* But to the majority of landowners, the life of the countryside—with its undifferentiated peasant masses, farming, the hunt, visits from relatives—still seemed adequate, even honorable.

For a young man so alive to the workings of others, Tolstoy's tender emotions and his eye for detail developed together, and there was much to see, much for him to immerse himself in. The peasant women who nursed him, his Aunt Aline's deranged companion, the noblemen who hunted with his father, the tutors (and they were numerous) of French and German origin, the household servants, then about thirty in number, who shuffled through the house, some sleeping on the huge Dutch heating stoves or in the halls— Yasnaya Polyana had a collective group psyche—everyone participated.

Yuletide celebrations were freewheeling and giddy. The household servants came to the house dressed up in costumes and danced as an ancient retainer named Gregory played the fiddle. The Tolstoy children dressed too, sang irreverent songs at the piano, allowed themselves to be swept away by the sight of the servants dressed as goats or Turkish soldiers or bears. Theatricals were often performed in the evenings. The household servants, often as proprietary about Yasnaya Polyana as the Tolstoys, played a huge and instructive role in Lev Nikolayevich's life. He describes the lulling pleasure of being with the housekeeper, Praskovya Issayevna:

> I remember one of the pleasantest impressions was that of sitting in her room after or during a lesson and talking with and listening to her . . . "Praskovya Issayevna, how did grandfather fight? On horseback?" one would ask her.
>
> "He fought in various ways, on horseback and on foot, and in consequence he was General-in-Chief," she would answer, opening a cupboard and getting out a burning tablet [a scented stick] which she called the Ochakovsky Smoke.
>
> According to her words, it appeared that this tablet grandfather brought from Ochakof. She would ignite a taper at the little lamp in front of the icons, and with it would light the tablet which would smoulder with a pleasant scent. She was connected in my eyes with the mysterious side of my grandfather's life.[11]

Servants served generations. At Yasnaya Polyana, despite differences in station, theirs was an intimate connection, in birth and death. "I remember," Tolstoy recalls, "how he died [the husband of his nurse], painfully, quietly, and meekly." Such memories remained at the very center of Leo Tolstoy's consciousness, grew to form the cornerstone of his thinking in later life. "The impressions of early childhood," wrote Tolstoy well before Freud, "grow in some unfathomed depth of the soul, like seeds thrown down on the ground, and after many years all of a sudden thrust their vernal shoots into God's world."[12]

The vernal shoots from Tolstoy's childhood were to grow to shake an entire continent. In his early days, no one would have guessed at this, but was there a clue to it in the character of a boy who wept when the stable boy was flogged?

In 1847, when Tolstoy came back from the University of Kazan to Yasnaya Polyana to live, he returned without his law degree, about which he had shown little enthusiasm, and with a bad case of venereal disease. In his diary he notes, "Now I ask myself, what will be the purpose of my life in the country for the next two years?"[13] Aunt Toinette was there to receive him, and he

This wing of the old house was to become the main house for Tolstoy after 1855. Seen here from the lower meadow.

records that they played duets together on the piano. Enchanting activity as this was, it was not what was driving Tolstoy at the time. Women, particularly Gypsy women, stirred in him an animal appetite. Alert to the running of his passions, he kept a diary of rules and admonishments, all calculated to rein him in and encourage a kind of pristine self-improvement. A sample: "Draw up a plan of everything you are studying and learn it by heart. Learn some poems each day in a language you are weak in." And: "Rules for developing physical activity: Think up as many occupations as possible for yourself."[14]

On April 19, 1847 he noted: "First rule. Keep away from women. Second rule. Mortify your desires by hard work." From the serf women on the estate came the temptation of carnal corruption (and purification), which was never-ending. "Oh it is difficult for a man to develop what is good in him under the sole influence of what is bad," he added later.

What a biographer learns about Tolstoy is that there was no "sole influence." He was too varied a creature, and if women tormented him he tended to pray for resistance, give in, admonish himself, and then go settle down and read Dickens or Rousseau, both of whom he describes as having an "immense influence" on him. Throughout his life, his sexual desire was to prove almost impossible to curb, although, being Tolstoy, he did try—through mental exercises, immersion in physical labor, or by calling up images of his mother.

It should be noted that Russian society at that time encouraged free-wheeling behaviors on the part of the young gentry, so he was right in the mainstream of things. Gambling at cards, often for days on end, elaborate food and drink, the leisurely pursuit of sexual pleasure—these were the givens of the upper classes. Most noblemen had sexual relations with one or two of the young serf women (Tolstoy no exception here), and it was considered a sign of virility to produce an occasional illegitimate child (Tolstoy had one illegitimate child, Timofey), the real object being to marry a rich woman after wild oats had been sown. His Aunt Toinette—"the purest of beings"—urged him to seek a relationship with a married woman of good breeding, though there is no record of his having reached this nirvana.

"I am writing you this letter from St. Petersburg, where I intend to remain *forever* [Tolstoy's italics]," he wrote his brother in February of 1848.[15] The next few years in the life of Tolstoy were spent in a series of sporadic stays at Yasnaya Polyana. "It was pleasant to live in the country with my aunt," he confided to a friend, "but a vain thirst for knowledge again called me away."[16] Knowledge, or perhaps the need for a little action.

From St. Petersburg he debated joining the war against Hungary—Russia had invaded Hungary in 1849—or finishing his law studies. He whipped through his two law exams, then jumped into the world of St. Petersburg society, where the lure of worldly pleasures, Gypsies, and card-playing snared him.

"I have done nothing necessary, only spent a heap of money and run up debts. Stupid! Insufferably stupid," he wrote again to his brother. Up all night gambling, he did in fact run up a pile of debts. "I am now without a penny at my disposal," he added, in what was surely an exaggeration of his plight. After each round of high living he thrashed about, full of self-admonishment. "Please God I will some day amend myself and become a respectable man."[17] Then in a chastened mood and laden with good resolve, he would hie it back to Yasnaya Polyana and take up the work of a landowner. For a time. In a clear-eyed moment he wrote, "I would be the unhappiest of men if I could not find a purpose for my life."[18]

In 1850 Tolstoy joined his brothers in Moscow. During this time, he kept his diary and tried a little writing, but his life seemed to swing between the poles offered by the monklike asceticism of Dmitri or the high self-indulgence of Sergei. Like many of his fellow noblemen, his passion for gambling was given full rein.

Back at Yasnaya Polyana in February of 1851, he records: "I've lost a lot of time. At first I was attracted by worldly pleasures, but then I felt empty at heart again . . . For a long time I was tormented by the fact that I had no heartfelt thought or feeling to determine the whole direction for my life—but now I think I have found a permanent aim—the development of the will—an aim toward which I've long been striving but which I only now recognize."[19] The development of the will was actually something of an old saw for Tolstoy, but one cannot fail to be touched by his feeling empty at heart. He was twenty-three. At loose ends. Without the much-sought-after purpose. Yasnaya Polyana was confining and could not soothe him.

Relief was in sight. His favorite brother, Nikolai, serving in the army, proposed that the restless Lev join him on a trip through the Caucasus.

> The Caucasus lies at my feet.
> I stand alone above the snows
> On edge of sheer abyss;
> From far off towering peak,
> An eagle takes its flight . . .

These lines of Pushkin begin a description of the Caucasus, but the eagle that takes its flight might well be Leo Tolstoy.

The mountainous Caucasus, in the southern part of Georgia, was almost designed to free a young nobleman of his ennui. Wildly beautiful, with steep, white cliffs and deep ravines, the Caucasus was populated with simple, primitive, virile tribesmen and dark-eyed women. Tolstoy joined in battle skirmishes, took endless walks, boated on the Volga River. He threw aside the chains of moral perfection (temporarily) and roamed, lighthearted and remorseless, through the mountains with Nikolai. He played chess with other officers long into the night. He gave in to sensuality. And everything *affected* him. "I was sitting by the window of my hut in Starogladkovsksys and revelling in nature with all my senses except touch. The moon had not yet risen . . . frogs and crickets merged together into one vague, monotonous nighttime

Tolstoy in uniform, photo-graphed 1856.

sound . . . I don't know how recollections of nights of Gypsy revelling have strayed into my roving imagination. Katya's songs, eyes, smiles, breasts, and tender words are still fresh in my memory, so why write them down?"[20]

Or, perhaps, why not write them down? But were words too trivial to describe his feelings?

> . . . from near the village came the sound of Tatars shouting and a dog barking; then again all was still, and I could hear nothing but the chirping of a cricket, and see a light, transparent cloud drifting past near the distant stars.
>
> I thought: I'll go and describe what I can see. But how can I write it down? I'll have to go and sit at an ink stained table, take out some drab coloured paper and ink, get my fingers dirty and draw letters on the paper. Letters make words, and words, sen-

tences; but can one really convey feeling? Is it ever possible to transmit to another person one's own views when contemplating nature? Description is not enough. Why is poetry so closely allied with prose, happiness with unhappiness? How ought one to live? Should one try to combine poetry and prose together, or enjoy one and take to living at the mercy of the other?[21]

He began writing *Childhood*. A purpose had been found.

2

SOLDIER, TEACHER, AND A TERRIFYING HAPPINESS [1852-1862]

"I have read your manuscript. Without knowing the sequel, I cannot make any final judgement, but it seems to me that the author has talent. In any case his ideas, and the simplicity and reality of his subject, form the unquestionable qualities of this work. If, as is to be expected, the sequel contains more animation and action, it will be a fine novel. Do send me the following sections. Your novel and your talent interest me. I advise you not to hide behind initials, but immediately to begin publishing under your real name, unless you are only a bird of passage on the literary scene. I await your reply."

Thus wrote N. P. Nekrasov, editor of the literary magazine *Sovremennik* ("*The Contemporary*") to an exhilarated LNT (he had signed the manuscript with only his initials) in the Caucasus in August of 1852.[1]

By November of 1853 Russia was at war with Turkey; the following March, France and England in turn declared war on Russia. Tolstoy by then had signed up for the regular army and had been made a lieutenant. His patriotic fever was up. He received an appointment to join the army in Romania, later was transferred to the Crimea, and on November 7, 1854, he arrived in Sebastopol for permanent duty. The Crimean War, like the First World War some sixty years later, was fought in the trenches. Thousands died for the capture of a hundred yards or so. In Sebastopol, from 1854 to 1856, Tolstoy faced the raw dangers of war. He served in the artillery, and accounts suggest that he fought bravely, often resubmitting himself to the battle lines, exposed to fire.

As well, he observed. He saw war with his own eyes. He took notes. His diary, April 1855: "The day before yesterday I spent the night in the 4th bastion. From time to time a ship fires on the town. Yesterday a shell fell near a boy and a girl who were playing horses in the street; they put their arms around each other and fell down together."[2] No longer could the world of war be pictured as a glorious enterprise, a game of wits between opposing generals. He was stunned by the cruelty of the officers toward their men. A soldier was flogged for scratching himself, another for smoking a pipe. The simple soldier lived under frightful conditions and was badly equipped. Indignant, and confident of being heard, Count Tolstoy wrote letters to the archduke demanding reform of the entire military machine. But more than anything else, Tolstoy was stirred by the heroism of the defenders of Sebastopol. He admitted, "War has always interested me."

He seemed to need to live on the edge of personal disaster off the

The village of Yasnaya Polyana in the summer.

battlefield, for throughout this period Tolstoy continued to gamble wildly—in the tradition of his class, to be sure—but he lost a fistful of money at cards.

But he also continued to write, which is harder to imagine, for the war zone proved to be a place of some productivity. Just before the outbreak of the war, *Childhood* was published in St. Petersburg by *The Contemporary*. The short novel was well received. Ivan Turgenev expressed admiration. "This is a sure gift. Write him and encourage him to continue." The editor, Nekrasov, asked for more stories. Thus *The Raid* was published in 1853, *Boyhood* in 1854, and on the bloody fields of Sebastopol, Leo Tolstoy wrote *Youth* and began *The Sebastopol Tales*.

No one wrote about war better than Tolstoy. These stories from the Sebastopol front are gentle and ironic in the narrative but etched in flesh and blood, dark emotions, and an extraordinary sense of what it felt like to serve on night duty at the bastion or to be swept up in the vanity of being an officer. *The Sebastopol Sketches*, as they were called, did run afoul of the government censor, a much-utilized tool of the monarchy. Tolstoy was angered by the inefficiency of the military and the amour propre of the officers; this is made vivid in the stories. But his patriotism was fierce, and the pieces were, for the most part, allowed through. Published in *The Contemporary* in 1855, *The Sebastopol Tales* proved to be a big hit. It has been suggested that Leo Tolstoy was the first real war correspondent.

He found time, too, to make long and painful entries in his diary: "I am ugly, awkward, and lack social education. I am irritable, a bore to others, not modest, intolerant and as shame-faced as a child. I am almost an ignoramus." In many of his bouts of self-examination, he tended to near comic injustice (an ignoramus?), but he could also see himself more reasonably at times: "I am clever, but my cleverness has as yet not been tested on anything."

But he did think about man's destiny, particularly his own destiny, and he remained absorbed with thoughts about religion. In March of 1855 he entered this in his diary:

"A conversation about Divinity and Faith has suggested to me a great, a stupendous idea, to the realization of which I feel myself capable of devoting my life. This idea is the founding of a new religion corresponding to the present state of mankind; the religion of Christianity, but purged of dogmas and mysticism; a practical religion, not promising future bliss, but giving bliss on earth. I understand that to accomplish this, the conscious labor of generations will be needed . . . Deliberately to promote the union of mankind by religion—that is the basic thought which, I hope, will dominate me."[3] He was twenty-six at the time.

A quiet but clearly troubling entry for the same year, 1855: "Played shtoss [a card game] for two days and nights. The result is understandable—the loss of everything—the Yasnaya Polyana house. I think there is no point in writing.—I'm so disgusted with myself that I'd like to forget about my existence."[4] His gambling debts had piled up to the point of madness, and the result was disastrous. For the relatively small price of five thousand roubles, the center section of the house at Yasnaya Polyana, the most elaborate part, with balconies and sweeping staircases, was literally cut out from the remaining two side wings, taken off in pieces, and reestablished on the estate of the new owner in the nearby town of Dolgoye. Tolstoy wrote to his beloved brother Nikolai, from whom loans had been solicited, begging forgiveness, continuing to blame his own stupidity.

Knowing what we do about Tolstoy's binding affection for Yasnaya Polyana, his diary entries for his gambling days in January of 1855 seem short and strangely lacking in the wild self-recrimination that he reserved, in page after page, for anguish over his sexual torment and "impurity." His humiliation must have been terrible. Yet, with half his house sold and carted off, the reformers' spirit, so much a part of his later reference, had still not found its way to his gambling habit. A week or so after the disastrous two-day shtoss binge, he confessed, "Played cards again and lost 200 roubles." The house at Yasnaya Polyana was reconstructed. His salad days were costly.

Ivan Turgenev, whose work had already achieved public acclaim, wrote to a friend from his estate at Spasskoye: "Tolstoy's article about Sebastopol [*The Sebastopol Tales*] is a gem. Tears came to my eyes as I read it, and I shouted Hurrah!"[5] So, although Tolstoy's personal habits continued to spiral out of control, his hand moved steadily across the page. And then—oh how he desired it—recognition! Not only from friends but from a larger public, a small ground swell of praise. The readership of *The Contemporary* numbered around twenty thousand at that time, and *The Sebastopol Tales* established him throughout Russian society as a writer of great promise. Even the tsar was reportedly enthusiastic about these tales from the front. "You are young," wrote Nekrasov, his enthusiastic editor, "changes are taking place which, let us hope, may end well, and perhaps a wide field lies before you."[6] The war ended with the defeat of Sebastopol, and Russia stood in need of reform. Tolstoy made his way to St. Petersburg and to a now quite curious circle of his admirers at *The Contemporary*.

He found the city of St. Petersburg in good spirits. The dispiriting war was over, and, more importantly, Nicholas I, a despotic monarch, had died in May of that year; he was succeeded by Alexander II, later known as the Tsar Liberator. In both the peasantry and the intelligentsia a new mood of hope could be felt, one which clearly anticipated the emancipation of the serfs. More freedom of expression was expected. Excitement was in the air; the stagnation of past decades was over. Turgenev, a man of warmth and elegance, welcomed Tolstoy, took him into his house, and with paternal zeal introduced him to an eager group of writers.

At first, the literati found the soldier who wrote from the field to be charming, although Turgenev did note his "barbaric odor and bullheadedness." Tolstoy grew increasingly uncomfortable among what he considered to be this group of bourgeois intellectuals, and over the next few weeks he began to quarrel with almost everyone—Goncharov, Druzhinin, Ostrovsky. He offended Turgenev with scrappy, disrespectful remarks; heaped disdain on the reforms they all advocated; spoke in scathing, sarcastic tones at a dinner in his honor.

Bullheadedness.

As well, he did put in some time at the brothels. The siren call of Gypsy women had not lessened for him. The result was that he was often up all night, sometimes two or three nights running, which made him a difficult house guest.

During this high-spirited winter, in the salons and the journals of St. Petersburg, arguments flew between the Slavophiles, advocates of the creed of uniqueness and superiority of the Russian spirit and traditions, and the "Westerners," who considered Russia a backward land in need of European influence. Tolstoy had moments when he felt alliance with the Slavophiles, but on balance he had contempt for both groups. They were, he felt, narrow and artificial, and he said so. The Slavophiles were too tied to Orthodox religion, the Westerners were just plain bourgeois. Just to keep things moving, he also attacked Shakespeare, Homer, and the brilliant Alexander Herzen, an early, renowned contributor to *The Contemporary*. What could come to the rescue of this unpleasant situation?

View of the estate, Tolstoy in the foreground. Behind him are peasant huts, the stables, and Volkonsky House, built by his grandfather.

A return to Yasnaya Polyana. Suddenly he was famished for the countryside.

In May of 1856, Tolstoy left St. Petersburg and tore home to Yasnaya Polyana. During the next months he tried to immerse himself in the estate and in his reading. Most people expected the emancipation of the serfs within the next few years. Tolstoy decided to make his serfs an early offer of his own: They would have immediate freedom and a complicated plan which consisted of their leasing, at a small price, the land over a period of years. But the serfs, crafty in their way, rejected the offer. With their long history of trusting the tsar ("the little father"), the muzhiks preferred to wait for *his* plan, which promised freedom *and* property outright. Tolstoy was furious. And bitterly disappointed. He had hoped to steal the march on the tsar.

And the new arrangement of the main house—or what was left of it—was awkward. The center of the old structure had been removed by the new owner, a man named Gorokhov, leaving behind a definite feel of recent, raw, architectural surgery. The two wings which remained, square and reasonably dignified, were now separated by empty space, a string of bushes, and what was left of the old stone foundation. Tolstoy and Aunt Toinette were now in one of the wings, and although all the old portraits had been re-mounted, the place seemed bleak and lacked the host of memories which Leo Tolstoy so needed. He put some time in on his novel, *The Cossacks,* and lusted, "to the point of physical illness."

Manorial life during this period was not without distractions. The joys of the hunt were constant, and Tolstoy was a passionate hunter. He formed a small music group, at which he played the piano. There was always a ball or two on one of the neighboring estates. He wrote a splendid short story, "Three Deaths," and felt occasional bursts of religious intensity. And the life of Yasnaya Polyana always engaged him. Yet, Tolstoy wrote, he "rode out with the dogs, but didn't find anything and was bored. Dined alone . . . As for my own writing, I've decided that my chief fault is timidity. I must be bold . . . Slept badly, sensual excitement."[7]

He felt, oddly enough, that his youth was over. Despite the erotic sat-isfactions of his affair with his serf-mistress Aksinia, he was lonely. As he walked through his orchards, smelled the spring lime trees, or made his way back to his very quiet house after a long ride, he was alone and he felt it. Knowing that the emancipation was due, Tolstoy began to take an interest in the education of the peasants. But one senses through this period a certain

Peasant with his plough.

melancholy, a feeling that he was just treading water. He fell in love with Valeriya Arsenyev, a young girl from a neighboring estate, but decided, after much backing and filling, that she had "no backbone or fire—just like noodles."[8]

His brother Nikolai described another side of Tolstoy's activities at Yasnaya Polyana during this time: "Lyovotchka is zealously trying to become acquainted with peasant life and with farming, both of which, like the rest of us, he has till now had but a superficial knowledge. Lyovotchka is delighted with the way the serf Ufan sticks out his arms when ploughing; and so Ufan has become for him an emblem of village strength, like the legendary Michael; and he himself, sticking his elbows out wide, takes to the plough and 'Ufanizes'."[9]

Still it was not enough. The work of the plough could not hold the restless Tolstoy. Over the next four years he traveled twice to Europe, the first trip (with Turgenev, with whom he was humbly reconciled) to Paris and Switzerland, the second, in 1860, to England and Germany. He visited European schools and found them to be suffocating. He fulfilled his role as an active tourist, but his interest in the state of things in "progressive" western Europe ended as quickly as it began. He decided that Europe was degenerate.

Then once again, the specter of death. His dearest brother, Nikolai, died of tuberculosis in Hyères, France. Tolstoy was at his bedside. Nothing in his life had ever produced such a strong impression on him. "What should one worry about or strive for when nothing remains of what was once Nikolai Tolstoy?" He asked himself, "If *he* found nothing to cling to, what can I find? Still less!"[10] Again and again, Why? Nikolai, who had neither had a chance to live nor understood the reasons for his death. After a bit more wandering, Tolstoy returned home and vowed to settle in at Yasnaya Polyana. The emancipation of the serfs had taken place quietly. The French philosopher Proudhon told him, "The future belongs to you Russians."

Leo Tolstoy never left Russia again.

"The pupil brings nothing to the classroom but himself, his rational mind, and the certainty that school will be as jolly today as it was yesterday."[11] Thus Tolstoy embarked on a new passion—the education of the peasant children of his estate. Who was in charge? He was. Established before his second trip to Europe and continued more vigorously after his return, the schoolhouse at Yasnaya Polyana held his attention (off and on) for the three years before his marriage.

Outraged by the state schools (few though they were) for the peasant children, where rote learning and flogging were common, Leo Tolstoy took on another persona—that of schoolmaster. In this new role he swept aside all conventions and built his ambitions around the natural receptiveness of the "free" child. Well ahead of John Dewey, Tolstoy boldly introduced his own progressive school. A sign on the doorway read, "Do as you like." Here at last the sons and daughters of his former serfs would enjoy freedom from the restraint of rules and would pursue lessons, each at his own pace. The child would feel a new intimacy and closeness with his teacher, and his spirit would be made open to learning. In Germany Tolstoy had visited schools where he witnessed nothing but prayers and oppressive factual lessons. "Civilization" was the corruptor. He didn't care for "progress" either. Only the *natural* in man need be revealed. In that spirit he took on the cause of peasant education.

Tolstoy did not do things in small stages. Beginning in 1859, through 1861, this disciple of Rousseau sought nothing less than sweeping and complete educational reform. Now his love of the muzhiks flourished, and we see Tolstoy in a very characteristic posture—full of passionate zeal, conviction, grandiosity—and the timing was good for him. Discouraged by his writing (*Family Happiness* was published in 1859 and he called it an abomination), Tolstoy concluded that at this point he was mature and that writing novels was simply not the work of grown men.

"To write novels that are charming and entertaining to read at the age of thirty-one. I gasp at the thought," he wrote to a friend.[12]

He plunged in. The other wing of the old house was rebuilt, with open and airy schoolrooms, gymnastic bars and a botany room on the first floor, and a total of forty "scholars," as they were called, assembled under the new master's care. On nice days, the children and teacher sat outside on the grass. Give-and-take was highly informal—no books used—with time out for wrestling and games whenever the spirit moved. The hours were loose, beginning with the ringing of a bell at around eight o'clock and ending whenever the group ran out of steam—often the children spent the night in Tolstoy's study. No child was forced to listen. But you can be sure they did.

"A child or a man is receptive; and therefore to regard a merry spirit in school as an enemy or a hindrance, is the crudest of blunders," he announced.[13] The merry spirit thrived. More importantly, all of Tolstoy's contempt for authoritarian posturing, from state and church, found its mark as he swept aside the strict rules under which children had been educated.

Where young students had been reduced to a "state school of mind," he now encouraged those qualities which he himself found admirable—ability to express natural, spontaneous thought, freedom to develop the trusting state of mind in which real learning can take place. As well, and this surely broke with precedent, he would teach them *whatever it was that they might want to learn.* And in this freewheeling and warm atmosphere, they might come to their learning out of real desire instead of enforcement. He sought nothing less than to invent his own pedagogy.

"No one, probably, will deny that the best relation between a teacher and his pupils is a natural one, and that the opposite to a natural one is a compulsory one. If that be so, then the measure of all scholastic methods consists in the greater or lesser naturalness, and consequently in the less or more compulsion enjoyed. The less the children are compelled, the better is the method. I am glad that it is not necessary for me to prove this obvious point."[14] Most of nineteenth-century Europe might have found it necessary for him to prove this point, but Tolstoy roared on, unperturbed. "All instruction should be simply a reply to questions put by life," he added. In his classroom, his deep suspicion of history as an explanation for anything was played out as he told his students (no books) about the Russian victory in the 1812 war and described the battles in the Crimea and the Caucasus. The human side of war was what he talked about. A former student recalls, "Hardly a lad among us could help shuddering at the horror of his descriptions." Arguments, arithmetic, grammar, carpentry—one can only imagine what this must have been like for a child used to the Scriptures and being flogged with regularity.

What was it like? Did they learn? An answer of sorts can be found in an article written by Vasily Stepanovich Morozov, a favorite student. He recalls:

> In three months time we were deep in our studies. By that time we could read with facility and the number of scholars had grown to seventy.
>
> All seventy of us would swoop down on Tolstoi, one with a question, another with a lesson book to show.
>
> "Lev Nikolayevich, is this right?"
>
> He would look at the book.
>
> "Yes, it's right, only you've left out something here. Otherwise it's fine. Don't hurry so."
>
> "What about mine—how do I write?" and another copy

book would be thrust under his nose, and then another, until the whole group was clamoring for his attention.

He would examine the books seriously and say a few kind words of approval sprinkled with remarks like:

"You'll have to rewrite that. You've left out too much."

In another room, that of the third form, a mistake was made. Someone, repeating the syllable "dra," omitted the "r."

"No, no that's wrong!" Lev Nikolayevich called out sharply, dropping the copying book he was examining. "No, no, that will never do!" And he hurried to the third form, enunciating the syllable on the way:

"D-r-a. What sound does that make?"

We answered in unison: "Dra."

His enthusiasm was catching, and our spirits rose with every new day. At noon, lunch was served. That was also the time for games and fun.

"How about a bite to eat and a whiff of fresh air?" Lev Nikolayevich would ask. "I'd like it too. Well, let's see who can get outside the fastest."

And all of us would rush, a shouting squealing horde, down the stairs at his heels. He took four steps at a time and easily outdistanced us. But we were never far behind.

"I'll be back in a jiffy," he'd say on reaching the wing of the next building, which was the house he lived in.

We would scatter down all the garden paths. Soon he would reappear. Followed more games, noise, shouting, running, throwing one another down in the snow and pelting one another with snowballs.

"Come on everybody, at me! Who can knock me down?"

We surrounded Lev Nikolayevich, clutched at him, tried to trip him, threw snowballs at him, sprang upon him, climbed up his back.

In such a happy atmosphere we made rapid strides in our studies and became very close to Lev Nikolayevich. We missed him when he was away, and he missed us. We were inseparable, parting only late at night. In the daytime we were together in

Tolstoy as schoolmaster during the height of his pedagogical activities, 1860.

school, in the evening we played together and sat on his verandah until midnight.[15]

One might ask, How was it that Lev Nikolayevich had such difficulties getting through dinner with his contemporaries in St. Petersburg and yet could spend carefree untroubled hours, day in and day out, with his little band of muzhik students?

Even his most serious detractors do not deny that he got along famously with children. And in his own lair, he was the undisputed center of attention. This group of young faces which surrounded him, waiting for his word, soothed his restless ego far better than could a few argumentative writers. As well, he was challenged by the young teachers he had hired (they were students or idealists who might, in our day, be called dropouts). He would form them, he decided; they would leave behind their ideas (or Herzen's) and become part of *his* philosophy. For the school at Yasnaya Polyana was utterly his. *His* onrush of creative energy, *his* thoughts put to the test. From all accounts the children genuinely loved him.

And Tolstoy, along with his youthful staff, wished to learn not only how to teach but what to teach. What are the proper subjects, he asked. Whatever the answers, he wanted to be proven right—always right. His underlying concern was to knock in the teeth those liberal "theoreticians" ("the Westerners") who felt called upon to lay their heavy hand on the peasants' education.

He expanded and organized other such schools in neighboring villages. The more significant expansion for Tolstoy was, however, the publication of the journal which he chose to call *Yasnaya Polyana*. (Was not the estate a place where natural man flourished—as opposed to the artificiality and modernism of the city?) The little monthly review was sent out more or less regularly. In it he described his activities and his thoughts (called, by some, propaganda) and often put in a piece of writing by one of the children. The publication was authorized by the official censor in January of 1862; soon it became clear that though it was rich in description, in its essential character the journal was quite political, a direct assault on the state and a challenge to the liberals, of whose overly intellectual and patronizing attitudes he was contemptuous.

It is hard to characterize Leo Tolstoy's politics at this time, particularly as he would argue that he didn't have any. Romain Rolland, the French biographer, has described Tolstoy as a revolutionary conservative. Because Tolstoy was constantly in the process of creating his own political philosophy, it's hard to give him a label. Boris Eikhenbaum, the well-known critic of the 1930s, suggests that, above all, Tolstoy was a man who believed in traditional, old values (based on the existing class structure) and, at the same time, sought to bring those values into a bold contemporary reality. But the important thing about this period in his life was that Tolstoy had begun a clearly political dialogue with the outside world. To start the school was one thing; to issue the journal, telling all about it, was the gauntlet thrown down.

To those of the twentieth century who have lived in the wake of John Dewey's thinking, Tolstoy's journal would not seem very provocative. Yet in Russia in the 1860s, despite the many pockets of revolutionary activity, state education was conducted in a rigid and stultifying manner. Sentences from his journal, such as, "He who is being taught must have full power to express his dissatisfaction," seemed designed to make the Ministry of Education jump.[16]

But Tolstoy's ultimate tussle was with the liberals at *The Contemporary*. Nikolai Chernyshevsky, the new editor, encouraged writers to serve radical political goals in their work. The nobleman from Yasnaya Polyana had been a suspect figure for some time, and now Chernyshevsky responded to the journal (after Tolstoy prodded him) by suggesting that he found Tolstoy's publication to be self-serving, archaistic, and, in his love for the peasant, "approaching folk-mysticism."

Twelve issues of the provocative little journal *Yasnaya Polyana* were published. A rumbling could be heard and the minister of the interior issued this report: ". . . I consider it necessary to direct your Excellency's attention to the general tendency and spirit of the magazine, which often infringes the fundamental rules of religion and morality. The evil lies in the falsity and . . . the eccentricity of those convictions, which being expounded with particular eloquence, may lead inexperienced pedagogues astray and give a wrong bias to popular education."[17]

The accusation of anarchism can be felt between the lines of this word from officialdom. Anarchism was often dealt with by swift exile.

Tolstoy's standing as a member of the ruling class would make him an interesting kind of anarchist. True, he was against all aspects of the existing order, but he had been born at the top of that order, as a member of the nobility. Of course, there was a tradition within the nobility of challenging the political status quo—the Decembrist revolt of 1825 was well remembered throughout Russian society, and by no one more than Tolstoy. But from the estate of Yasnaya Polyana a unique figure emerged. He did not seek attachment with his fellow nobility; he removed himself swiftly from the literary group, he claimed no politics, had almost no alliances. Yet, there he sat, outside the mainstream, as it were, secure and isolated at Yasnaya Polyana—and from there he fired his volleys. He did not speak for anyone, and God knows no one dared speak for him.

The dual role that the estate played in the logistics of this period of his life is important. Yasnaya Polyana protected him. He did not have to live with the daily give-and-take, and so-called trivia of the many reform movements. He could make a strategic retreat from St. Petersburg, away from the jittery literati; here was the countryside, the warmth of the main house, his undisputed role as head of state—all waiting for him. He could claim, as he did (and believed, for periods), to be only interested in returning to farming, to managing the property, perhaps writing a few stories.

And yet, it was here, in this dulcet countryside, that he developed his radicalism. The school served as a laboratory, the journal as a prod. From Moscow and St. Petersburg, letters flew back and forth, charges in newspapers, replies and countercharges. From the distance of his estate, coupled with

Winter view on the estate. This is what isolation looked like in rural Russia.

his stated disdain for politics, he could address political issues. In his way. With his "particular eloquence." From his own turf. In tennis, it might be known as having the server's advantage; the timing, the placement, and the speed of the opening shots were his.

As well, the fact of his possession of Yasnaya Polyana affected not just the logistics but the substance of the way he thought about things. Although he had begun to wear peasant garb, Tolstoy lived distinctly above the fray, without concerns for money and time. His degree of independence, in a time when most were engaged in struggle or servitude, was quite something to imagine. How could a man be so able to address the large concerns of a massive country, as he was beginning to do, yet be, in some sense, outside the main experience of the Russian population of his day?

His principal biographer and friend, the Englishman Aylmer Maude, suggests the following: "His independent position made easier the formation of that state of mind free from intellectual prejudice which enabled him, later on, to examine the claims of the Church, of the Bible, of the economists, of governments and the most firmly established manners and customs of society, untrammeled by the fear of shocking or hurting other people." His estate, Yasnaya Polyana, was the earthly symbol of this independent position. As long as he was there, who, in fact, could he shock? Tolstoy was not a figure at court, as so many noblemen were (as was his cousin Alexandra). He was not tied into the monarchy, although he claimed a certain familiarity. ("Dear Brother," he once addressed a letter to the tsar.) At Yasnaya Polyana, he had his own "clear glade," and at this point in his life he tended to ignore the Church and had more or less dismissed the literary set.

Maude continues: "I should say that Tolstoy had no adequate sense of being a responsible member of a complex community with the opinions and wishes of which it is necessary to reckon. On the contrary, his tendency was to recognize, with extraordinary vividness, a personal duty revealed by the working of his own conscience and intellect . . ."[18]

Thus he plunged on, Tolstoy, freed by his independence, his personal duty writ large on his heart, his moral urgency at that moment given its focus in the education of the peasants. He sat on his porch with his students from the Yasnaya Polyana school. Often, after lessons, he told them of his desire to divide up his land and live like a peasant, like them. He would marry a good peasant woman, and till the soil. The little scholars were disbelieving.

"We were all silent," recalls the former student Vasily Stepanovich. "Each of us tried to discover whether Lev Nikolayevich was serious or joking." And he adds, with the simple wisdom which Tolstoy himself revered, "As if one could turn a nobleman into a muzhik!"[19]

Tolstoy took off for Samara for a rest cure in July of 1862 and while he was gone an event took place that could not have been imagined. Yasnaya Polyana, left in the frail hands of Aunt Toinette, was the subject of a government raid. On the morning of July 6, the tsar's version of the KGB, called the "third section," arrived at Yasnaya Polyana in three troikas, wearing blue coats and rattling officialdom, and began a two-day search of the property for "subversive material." Since the publication of the journal, Tolstoy had been a suspect figure. Now drawers were flung open, books upended, papers rifled. Tolstoy's diary was read. They swooped down on the school, ripping open desks and pupils' notebooks, creating mayhem. Frustrated that they could find nothing, the blue-coated figures dragged the pond and lifted the floor up from the stable. The sum total of the subversive material found in a wracking two-day search was an old copy of Herzen's exile newspaper, *The Bell.*

The official report filed from the leader of the raid, Colonel Durnovo, states: "A search of Count Tolstoy's house revealed it to be very modestly furnished, containing no secret doors, hidden staircases or lithography stones or telegraph . . . Tolstoy is very haughty with his neighbors and has made enemies of the local landowners by systematically defending the muzhiks during his term as Arbiter of the Peace," Durnovo added, somewhat lamely.[20]

Tolstoy learned of this invasion on July 20 and was furious. He raced home to Yasnaya Polyana and fired off two scathing letters to his cousin Alexandra, a regular at court, in which he heaped scorn on the government and demanded an official apology and explanation. He threatened to leave Russia, which no one took seriously, kept pistols in his bedroom, and seemed restless and despondent. He felt, in addition to the wounded vanity of one whose sacred property has been violated, that the peasants had grown suspicious of him as a result of the raid. "The peasants no longer regard me as an honest man—an opinion I have earned over the course of the years—but a criminal."[21]

On his thirty-fourth birthday, August 28, 1862, weeks after the raid, he addressed himself thus in his diary: "Ugly mug! Do not think of marriage, your calling is of another kind."[22] This bleak mood was somewhat relieved by the promise of an official apology. Although the school at Yasnaya Polyana continued after this indignity, something in its master seemed to snap, to cause the enchantment with the school to end.

Or, perhaps, another enchantment had come to replace it.

After what could be described as a most practical (and unsuccessful) search for a wife, Tolstoy at last focused in on one family, that of his old childhood friend Lyubov Alexandrovna Behrs.

Three daughters took center stage in the Behrs household: Liza was twenty, Sonya eighteen, and the youngest, Tatyana, barely sixteen. Mme Behrs, an ambitious and orderly woman, hoped to marry off Liza first; she had Count Lev Nikolayevich in mind.

By this time Tolstoy's state of mind was one of genuine anxiety. For he had seen Liza, both in Moscow and at her uncle's country estate near Yasnaya. Beautiful as she was, he didn't feel the attraction for her that he knew was essential—but he did feel it for her younger sister Sonya. Yet he was troubled and uncertain of his own feelings. "What if this be only a desire for love and not real love? I try to notice her weak points, but yet I love."[23]

Two weeks later, he was in worse shape. "Lord! Help me and teach me. Another sleepless and agonizing night; I feel it, I, who laughed at the sufferings of people in love. What you laugh at, you become a slave to. How many plans have I made to tell her and Tanechka, and all in vain. I'm beginning to hate Liza with all my heart. Lord, help me, teach me. Mother of God, help me."[24]

Sonya was not the prettiest of the Behrs daughters, but she had a certain allure, a keenness, and luminous dark eyes. As well, she possessed a rich blend of emotions—she could be melancholy, joyous, jealous, reflective. She was smart, too, the only one of the daughters to earn a certificate in teaching. Lev Nikolayevich, in his fascination with her, decided to test her.

They were seated at a card table, and Tolstoy took a piece of chalk and wrote out some letters: y. y. & n. f. h. t. r. m. a. &. i. f. Random letters? Absolutely not. He asked her to fill in the sentence, based on these letters he then thrust toward her. She nodded, and, concentrating with all her powers, her face flushed, she completed his sentence: "Your youth and need for happiness too vividly remind me of my age and incapacity for happiness." She read it out loud. It was not the greatest Tolstoy sentence, but she had shown herself to be able to *decipher* him, to be in harmony with him. To be, perhaps, equal to him. In her diary she records the event as of great significance. Readers of *Anna Karenina* will see that Tolstoy also found it of great significance, for the exact scene is pictured vividly in Part 4, Chapter 11, as Levin courts his beloved Kitty.

Meanwhile, Liza Behrs, who in concert with her mother had set her cap for Tolstoy, was in despair, and her father, Dr. Behrs, was furious. Nonetheless, the parents did not wish to fly in the face of Sonya's happiness, and after an awkward afternoon, agreed to Tolstoy's proposal: He would marry Sonya, and in a week at that!

Sonya's name day, September 17, was celebrated with additional fervor. And Leo Tolstoy gave her what has to be considered a very dubious birthday present. He presented her with his diaries to read. He told her that he felt honor bound to keep nothing from her.

Honor was perhaps combined with the Tolstoy grandiosity; it proved a disastrous thing to do. Sins, hopes, self-castigation, references to his mistress Aksinia, depravity in St. Petersburg—it was there in page after page. It is possible to consider (as does Aylmer Maude) that the giving of the diaries was consistent with Russian tradition of confession followed by blessing. But

Sonya was crushed. His utterly specific, wide-ranging, and quite raunchy revelations about his relationships with women shocked her to the core. Indeed, the reading of the diary sparked in her an almost permanent jealousy, which was to plague this complicated union to its very last days.

As for Tolstoy, this diary-rendering was in character. He was a man of sweeping gestures—she must know him through and through—and in constant search of absolution—Would she forgive him?

She did. Later, they would exchange diaries, and this became a way in which they communicated with each other. But eighteen-year-old Sonya now approached marriage to a man who incited in her a combination of admiration and horror.

The wedding, attended by three hundred guests, started an hour late because Tolstoy couldn't find a clean shirt. But otherwise the ceremony, in the tradition of the Russian Orthodox church, was beautiful, with a hidden choir, the lighting of candles, and lovely chanting. Sonya wept throughout.

One could not help but feel that this couple of elegant bearing was off to a poor start—the tensions surrounding Liza, the diaries, the excessive weeping, the haste of it all.

But they had some good luck. The love they both hoped for blossomed.

"Incredible happiness," Tolstoy proclaimed in his diary, after their return to Yasnaya Polyana. "I can't understand how this week has passed. I don't remember anything; only the kiss by the piano . . ." Later: "I can't recognize myself. All my mistakes are clear to me. I love her just the same, if not more."[25] At Yasnaya Polyana, Sonya appeared to put behind her the nightmare of the week surrounding her marriage and allowed herself to be drawn into his passion for her. Her diary often reflected jealousy and morbidity—"I am terribly sad and take refuge in myself. My husband doesn't love me."[26] But she is quick to record her ardor as well: "I could die of happiness and humility in the presence of such a man . . . I love him to the uttermost limit with all my soul."[27]

In the gentle autumn at Yasnaya, they seemed to be able to turn their fascination with each other into a kind of bliss, replete, to be sure, with meteoric moods, quarrels, and grand reconciliations. Tolstoy's close friend, the poet A. A. Fet, visited and found them overflowing with happiness. And Sonya began to take charge of the meandering staff and sagging gardens. Clearly she enjoyed being Countess Tolstoy. She introduced Count Tolstoy to the refinement of sleeping on sheets. He preferred, previous to her arrival, a simple blanket and a leather pillow.

"Another month of happiness," he writes on December 19. "The features of my present life are fullness, absence of dreams, hopes and self-consciousness, but on the other hand fear and remorse over my own egotism. The students are leaving today and I'm sorry for them, Auntie has assumed a new, elderly expression which touches me."[28]

The students were leaving. The school had been carrying on without its major player, he was preoccupied with domestic bliss and now he decided that both the school and the journal were a burden. Later he would write to his favorite cousin Alexandra, by way of explanation: "I am glad that I passed through this school. This last mistress of mine had a great formative influence on me, but it is difficult for me to understand the way I was a year ago. The children come to me in the evenings and bring back memories of the teacher who used to be me and is no longer there."[29]

Sonya Behrs, during her first months as Countess Tolstoy.

Peasant shoemaker and his family.

His world was now filled with domestic happiness. Throughout the winter, he took Sonya on night sleigh rides—bundled her up in a huge fur rug and rode through the night with bells jingling. She learned to deal with the household servants. She took up her post at daily tea by the samovar. In fact, Sonya appeared to be able to satisfy Tolstoy's highly idealized view of what a wife should be. She was devoted to him, dedicated to the running of the estate, and had an innocent quality to her face which enchanted him. And she was pregnant. Nothing better could have happened to ensure her claim on his love than that she bear children.

Seized with a renewed energy, he plunged into the work of the estate, planting trees, starting a bee farm. But something else was building, a return to a calling which he had never really left but about which he had been scornful. A calm and assured Tolstoy was now ready to begin to write again. The school had not really been a departure but a stepping-stone, another creative act. In his diary he wrote, "A mass of thoughts. I just want to write. I've become terribly grown up."[30]

With the coming of Sonya, Tolstoy began a period in his life which he described as "internal emigration." He buried himself at Yasnaya Polyana. On March 8, 1863, he wrote to his sister: "I am a happy man; I live listening to a child kicking in Sonya's womb, I am writing a novel and some short stories, and I am getting ready to build a distillery."[31]

The distillery can be overlooked. The novel to which he refers is *War and Peace*.

3

WAR AND PEACE
[1862-1869]

In a letter once written to Aunt Toinette from the Caucasus, Tolstoy talked about Yasnaya Polyana and the life he dreamed of for himself on the estate. He spoke of the wife he would have, "gentle, kind and affectionate," of his brothers and sister and their families who would visit, of the "children who would call you Grandmaman." The continuation of life as it was designed, the fruitfulness of domestic happiness—this is what he pictured. His letter concluded, "If they made me Emperor of Russia or gave me Peru, in a word, if a fairy came in with her wand asking what I wished for—my hand on my conscience, I should reply that I only wish that this dream may become a reality."[1]

In fact, in some measure, by 1863, it had become a reality. Tolstoy's vision of Yasnaya Polyana was now well within reach. Aunt Toinette was secure in her old age; Sonya's pregnancy guaranteed a new generation. If the estate had fallen off a little in maintenance, it could now be infused with new energy, a new sense of propriety—more planting, a richer variety of animals (Japanese hogs were added), additional self-sufficiency. The serfs had been freed by decree, and yet life went on for most of them in the same rhythms of the past—seasons of planting and harvest, the celebration of holidays. After some wanderings, and some doubts, the life of Tolstoy the patriarch, now age thirty-five, was resumed in full measure.

At the core of the newfound order in his life was his marriage to Sonya. His diary entries about her seem to be written as if in a trance. "I love her still more and more. Today is the seventh month and I'm experiencing a feeling which I haven't experienced in a long time, not since the beginning—a feeling of nothingness compared to her. She is so impossibly pure and good and chaste for me. At times like this I feel as if I don't possess her, despite the fact that she gives herself completely to me."[2]

And Sonya, for her part, despite bouts of melancholy, writes to her sister Tanya: "We are very happy. Lyovochka is constantly avowing that he could never love me as much in Moscow as he does here."[3] Apparently Yasnaya Polyana brought out the best in him. She adds: "He really loves me. It's so frightening."

At first, she had trouble simply finding what it was she was supposed to do. Tolstoy was out all day dealing with the estate, and it took Sonya a while, but just a little while, to understand that she too could take charge. To be sure, she could always reorganize the linen, salt the cucumbers, and play a little piano, but Sonya was far too ambitious to be so confined. She too took to walking in the fields, a proprietary bunch of keys swinging at her waist. She learned, perhaps by default, the beginnings of the massive effort called book-keeping. Later, it was to become a particular domain of power for her. A son, Sergei, was born within the first year. If she missed the robust din of her brothers, safely back in Moscow, she began a life centered around children of her own. She records a "terrifying happiness."

Both principals in this complicated marriage were in the habit of wild mood swings. Tolstoy complained that he felt moral lassitude, that he slept poorly; due to this period of happiness he had stopped looking for the meaning of life. He could fall into despondency ("No, she never loved me . . .") and seconds later be full of rapturous happiness. The habit of diary exchanges continued to be dangerous.

Sonya was prone to be self-analytic. Complicated, somewhat morose reflections fill her diary. She did not share her husband's veneration of the serfs. ("He disgusts me with his People.") And as to his former serf-mistress, a wave of near-suicidal jealousy came over her when she saw Aksinia ("fat, pasty, horrible"), who continued to work in the main house. (This insensitivity was corrected.)

"Lyovochka and I have started working on the estate; he's taking it very seriously, I—more or less pretending to," she wrote in her diary, noting as well that it was all "joyful."[4] Later in a letter to her sister, she appears almost enthusiastic: "We are becoming quite the farmers. We are buying cattle, fowl, pigs and calves. I'll show you everything. Lyovochka and I long for the day of your arrival."[5]

In the spring Tolstoy immersed himself in the ploughing of the fields, a labor which lifted his spirits. He would often work tirelessly until dusk, then present himself at the evening table in his muddy boots and peasant shirt, smelling like a muzhik. The servants expected little else, but Sonya was stunned.

By summer, family began to appear at Yasnaya Polyana. Given the lack of railroads, and the Russian tradition of exuberant, open-ended hospitality, they often stayed for the whole season. When snow and the frozen mud on the roads gave way, they came. Family will visit, Tolstoy had said in his letter to Aunt Toinette. Indeed they did.

Sonya's brother Stepan spent every summer of his youth at Yasnaya Polyana. Tolstoy's older brother Sergei, though a near neighbor, came to stay. Friends, too. The poet A. A. Fet, an endearing, dreamy fellow, was, through these years at least, Tolstoy's principal confidant. Then there was Turgenev. Tolstoy both loved him and was irritated by him; they once staged a duel over very little. But he was, at this time, a constant visitor. Marya, Tolstoy's sister, stayed for months on end with her children.

Perhaps overshadowing all the others in the degree to which she integrated herself into the life at Yasnaya Polyana was Sonya's younger sister, Tanya Behrs.

She was not conventionally pretty, the enchanting Tanya. She had a mass of black hair, and big ears, but with her extraordinary smile and quick sense of humor, she seemed like a tonic designed to raise the spirits of everyone around her, particularly Sonya. In the evenings, with Tolstoy at the piano, she sang. Children instinctively wanted to be near her. She rode as well as most men and spent long hours hunting for woodcock with adored Lyovochka.

The tableau of family and friends grew; expeditions on horseback, mushroom gathering, and picnics carried everyone off for rapturous afternoons. Tolstoy, according to his sister-in-law Tanya, was engrossed in the farm, sheep pens, and his beekeeping operation but joined the merrymakers when he could. She noticed that he seemed preoccupied, often taking notes.

She asked him: "Why are you always writing in your little book?"

Peasant carpenters.

He smiled and said: "I'm taking notes about you."

"But what's interesting about us?"

"That's my concern. The truth is always interesting."[6]

Summer amusements continued on into the fall. Plays, one called *The Infected Family,* written in some haste by Tolstoy, were performed in the evenings and seemed to regale everybody. It was a time of family happiness, but it all had an additional meaning to Leo Tolstoy. Here was the triumph of the countryside over city life, the virtues of the natural world of the country pitted against the theorists and the salon thinkers and the "contrived" society of St. Petersburg. As the world would learn, domestic happiness and the manorial way of life was to serve as one of the major thematic preoccupations of *War and Peace.*

Why was he taking notes? *That's* why he was taking notes. In his mind, slowly, a work was forming, and they were all in it—Sonya, Sergei, his father, and Tanya.

"Girls, I'll tell you a secret which I beg you not to repeat," Sonya had warned her sisters in a letter, dated November 11, 1862. "Lyovochka may write about us when he reaches fifty."[7]

It happened well before he was fifty. In 1862 he was thirty-five, and in a letter to his cousin Alexandra he reported that he felt "powerful, capable of work."[8] He was restless ("I'm reading Goethe, and thoughts are swimming in my head") and impatient with himself for his collapse into domestic life, even though, of course, just this domestic tranquillity had allowed his writing to go forward. He handed over the management of the estate to Sonya and set to work.

For Tolstoy, unconscious preparation for a large historical novel had been at play for years. He could draw both from the legends of his family, intimately interwoven with Russian history, and the fruit of his earlier works: *Childhood; Youth,* self-involved but rich in detail; the war stories from Sebastopol which focused on the inner experience of the soldiers; and *The Cossacks,* celebrating the unbridled spirit of the free and natural man. These stories,

The study where War and Peace *was written. Note Tolstoy's scythe on the wall.*

splendid in their own right, still seemed to build, drawn like parts in a magnetic field, toward the epic of *War and Peace*.

It took this period of relative calm to allow the genius of Tolstoy loose to begin to form this new and massive work. His energy and imagination were focused on one of the great political legends of the nineteenth century: the Decembrist uprising.

Some thirty-seven years earlier, on December 14, 1825, a group of three thousand military officers and noblemen had gathered in front of the assembly in St. Petersburg demanding constitutional reform. An amalgam of "repentant noblemen," writers, intellectuals, Freemasons, and militia who were disenchanted with the monarchy, they were poorly organized. After a series of unanswered demands, saber rattlings, and futile negotiations, Tsar Nicholas I, unsure as to how to deal with them (for they were, after all, in some sense his own social class), finally opened fire on them in Senate Square. The Decembrist Revolution, frail as it was, was over. The monarchy, shaken, tightened its grip.

Tolstoy had long been intrigued with the story of the Decembrists. Called the revolution of the nobility, the small uprising had become a political legend. Self-sacrifice, idealism, the ambivalence within the tradition (his tradition) of the repentant noblemen—all served to connect him to the Decembrists. And among those heroic revolutionaries later tried and sent into exile in Siberia was Major General (Prince) Sergei Grigoryevich Volkonsky, a relative of Tolstoy's mother.

Thus Tolstoy began to write the story of one Decembrist revolutionary who returns from exile with his family to find a new Russia. And it was to be a novel, not a perpetration of the legend of the upper-class revolt. Tolstoy said at the time, "No matter how much I might want to present my readers with a Decembrist hero who is above all weakness, to be perfectly truthful I must admit that Pytor Ivanich shaved with extreme care, combed his hair, and looked at himself in the mirror."[9] He had surely caught the flavor of the moment, for, as one critic suggested, the Decembrists had a saber in one hand and a glass of claret in the other.

Tolstoy completed three chapters of *The Decembrists*. Egged on by a challenge from his old nemesis *The Contemporary,* in whose pages the editors had hinted that the literary career of Tolstoy was over, he sought to produce a novel which would stand as a response to political rumbling and contemporaneity—a novel of flesh and blood and history.

But something happened to this first plan. As most of the Decembrists had been deeply involved in the War of 1812, in seeking the origins of their idealism Tolstoy had to go back to that period, "a period whose scent and sound are still perceptible to us." Thus he retrenched. The novel would begin in and around 1812. But reason suggested that in order to fully comprehend the patriotic war of 1812 in which Russia eventually did triumph, he must investigate the war and period surrounding the earlier defeat, in 1805, at the hands of Napoleon's armies.

Thus another retrenching to 1805. And in the doing, the Decembrists were abandoned. Boris Eikhenbaum suggests that Tolstoy might have felt that the language of the first three chapters of *The Decembrists,* that of journalistic prose, lacked "personality." This is an interesting thought, particularly when one considers the lighthearted, whimsical, domestic style of some of the language of the final *War and Peace.* He was still searching.

During this period one observes a Tolstoy who is both comfortable with his world and working at his fullest powers. He spent most of the spring of 1864 conducting a massive search through letters and historical documents (many of whose chronology he later ignored). Urged on by his father-in-law, Dr. Behrs, who sent him batches of documents from Moscow, Tolstoy now conceived a novel which, at its core, would describe the collision between family life among the landed gentry and the great war of 1812.

By September of 1864, the first chapters of the novel, now titled *The Year 1805,* were in full swing. Tolstoy had decided that the politics and descriptions of historical events would serve only as a background to the domestic life of his characters. The social structure and emotional life of his gentry families, the Rostovs and the Bolkonskys, in other words the peace of *War and Peace,* was at this time set to dominate the novel.

A hunting accident—he was thrown from his horse while trying to jump a ravine—caused a dislocated shoulder and right arm and pitched him, literally, into the arms of his in-laws, the Behrs. Incompetent local doctors (with the aid of two sturdy peasants and a bottle of chloroform) failed to reset the arm properly and Dr. Behrs summoned his son-in-law to Moscow for more exacting surgery.

Once the surgery was completed, Tolstoy was urged to recover in Moscow under the watchful eye of Dr. Behrs. He was desperate to write, to keep the novel going, yet his arm hung in a sling. Sonya was back at Yasnaya

Polyana, heavily pregnant, awaiting their second child. At the Behrs's lovely apartment, eager to attend to his every need, sat her sisters, Tanya and Liza (once heartbroken, now recovered). He began to dictate.

Tanya remembers:

> In the days after his operation he dictated to me letters to Sonya and part of the novel, *1805,* that is *War and Peace.* I see him clearly . . . with a look of concentration on his face, supporting his injured arm with his other hand—walking back and forth dictating. Ignoring me completely, he talked aloud: "No, a cliche won't do," or he simply said, "Strike that out."
>
> His tone was commanding. There was impatience in his voice, and often while dictating he would change a passage some three or four times . . . I had the feeling that I was doing something immodest, that I was being an involuntary witness to his inner world, hidden from me and from everyone.[10]

Dr. Behrs persuaded Tolstoy to give a reading from the novel, a reading to be held in the living room of the Perfilyevs, an old, most traditional Moscow family. Again, Tanya sets the scene:

"A few friends had gathered at the Perfilyevs'. The preparations for the reading suggested some solemn occasion, like the preparations for a christening. Nastasya Sergeyevna, wearing a high cap, sat on a large mahogany divan with a tall straight back. Papa sat next to her. When everyone was seated, Lyovochka began to read. He started rather uncertainly, as if embarrassed. I was scared—all is lost, I thought. Then somehow he regained assurance, read with such strength, so captivatingly that I felt he carried us all away. And I wanted to cry out, 'I'm in a whirl, a whirl!' "[11]

It is important to note that, as well as putting a few pages on the novel, in these weeks of recuperation Tolstoy found a huge and infinitely valuable resource: the Behrs family. His special fondness for Tanya is complex—there are some who believe that he was, fleetingly, in love with her. She is clearly the model for the central character of the novel, Natasha Rostov. Liza Behrs scoured libraries and found references for her brother-in-law, and Dr. Behrs, a man of vitality, urged him forward on all fronts. Mme Behrs remained pretty much indisposed, but the family, Sonya's family, became his. He loved her brothers. He needed them all. His parents and two of his brothers were dead.

The zala, the main room that served as both dining and living rooms. This corner, Tolstoy's favorite, came to be called the "Serious Talk" corner.

And in his effort to bring the richness of family life to the pages of *War and Peace,* were they not an ideal family?

At home, back at Yasnaya Polyana, everyone seemed to leap into the process of Tolstoy's writing. Copying, readings, a bit of research—this pattern, spearheaded by Sonya, was established at Yasnaya Polyana, the place where most of *War and Peace* was written.

It is at this time, when this extraordinary and unwieldy epic was being written, that Sonya, Countess Tolstoy, found a real niche for herself. Among the Tolstoy biographers, one can find some division of alliance concerning the marriage of the Tolstoys, particularly surrounding the question of which of them was at fault for the quite disastrous final years. But no biographer fails to acknowledge the invaluable role that Sonya played in the early years when Tolstoy's fiction flourished. For she flourished with it. This young bride, who bore children almost continuously from 1862 to 1881, found profound satisfaction in the work of his aide-de-camp. She copied and recopied, criticized, edited, corrected—and then did it all over again. In his *Reminiscences,* their son Ilya recalls:

The parlor, just off the zala, where Sonya copied War and Peace.

"She used to sit in her small drawing room off the zala* at her little writing table, and spend all her free time writing. Leaning over the manuscript and trying to decipher my Father's scrawl with her short-sighted eyes, she used to spend whole evenings at work, and often stayed up late at night after everyone else had gone to bed. He had very bad handwriting and a terrible habit of inserting whole sentences between the lines, or in corners of the page, or sometimes right across it. My mother often discovered gross grammatical errors, and pointed them out to my father and corrected them."[12]

The work of the editors surrounding the passionate work of Tolstoy (Tanya joined the effort) during the summer of 1865 established Yasnaya Polyana as a center of literary activity. *War and Peace,* with its intensity of immediately felt experience, was at the core of life at Yasnaya Polyana, with *its* intensity of immediately felt experience. In his memoirs, Ilya Tolstoy offers the calculation that, through the din of visitors, nursery noises, and large family

* The large, second-floor dining room, which also served as the main gathering place in the evenings.

meals, Sonya copied out the whole of *War and Peace* by hand a total of seven times. A staggering thought.

The work of the copyist was enlivened by a game which indeed might have enchanted us all. In the theater of this great work (by 1866 titled, unfortunately but briefly, *All's Well That Ends Well*) are more than five hundred characters. Among the principals, perhaps a dozen or so, could be found likenesses of Tolstoy family members. Who was who?

Was not Princess Marya Bolkonsky modeled after Princess Marya Volkonsky, Tolstoy's mother, or at least his vision of her? And old Prince Bolkonsky is undoubtedly rooted in Grandfather Volkonsky. Tolstoy changed but one letter of the names. Prince Andrei, whose death scene is one of the most powerful in all literature, does he not bear resemblance to Tolstoy's aristocratic brother Sergei? Nicholas Rostov is loosely based on Tolstoy's father, with his love of hunting and heightened sense of honor. And easy to recognize, in the central figure of Natasha Rostov, is, of course, Tanya. Jubilant, life-affirming Tanya. In his later public pronouncements, Tolstoy suggested that Natasha was a creature based on both Sonya and Tanya. Perhaps Sonya is represented more accurately in the final chapters, when we see Natasha after the war, married, a mother of children, as life returns to familiar patterns.

While family and friends enjoyed the game of spotting each other in scene after scene, Tolstoy was busy writing the greatest work in Russian literature. The book assumed a kind of colossal structure, full of digressions, flights of imagination, personal memories, and pronouncements. He created characters—Prince Andrei, Pierre, and Natasha—who would live on, outside the borders of the story. As to the complex form of the book—well, it was "designed to suit what the author had to say," he announced in a later article.

Then, as now, no one was quite sure what to call *War and Peace,* with its length and breadth and history and fiction and philosophizing all rolled into one. Tolstoy himself resisted a label. It is not, in conventional terms, a novel, although it is often billed as such. An epic, of course, by its length and sweep alone, but perhaps it is an idyll, a journey through time. It has been suggested that it is a historical chronicle except that the history is often purposely rearranged. Created fictional characters like Prince Andrei mingle with well-known real characters such as Napoleon and General Kutuzov. The battles of Austerlitz and Borodino are recorded with a passion and detail previously unknown in war annals. But Tolstoy steps outside the narrative and uses these

Ivan Turgenev.

scenes to suggest a new philosophy of history. *War and Peace* defies classification; it is, quite simply, independent of any conventional literary form.

"I simply love what is definite, clear, beautiful and unpretentious, . . ." Tolstoy wrote after the book was published.[13] He disliked the artistry thought to be necessary in writing and sought instead to create life in progress, "life in all of its countless and inexhaustible manifestations." And from Yasnaya Polyana he was able to take the countless, inexhaustible manifestations of his family circle of 1865, as well as his own obsessions, and transfer it all back fifty years to the time of *War and Peace.*

Once begun, the writing of the book went forward with furious intensity. He moved himself and his papers to a quiet room on the downstairs floor, formerly a pantry, and in February of 1865 the first installment, called *1805,* was published by *Russkii Vestnik* ("*Russian Herald*"), the first of a plan for six volumes. Tolstoy wrote to Fet:

> In a few days the first half of the first part of *1805* will be out. Please write and tell me your opinion in detail. I value your opinion and that of a man I dislike all the more the older I get, Turgenev. He *will understand.**

* Turgenev apparently did *not* understand, for he wrote: "It is a great mistake when a self educated man of Tolstoy's type starts to philosophize."[15]

What I have published in the past I consider a mere trial of the pen, a rough draft. What I am publishing now, although I like it more than my previous work, still seems weak—as an introduction is bound to be. But what is to follow will be—tremendous!! Write and tell me what they say about it in the various places you know, and particularly its effect on the masses.[14]

The first reviews of *1805* were what is politely known as "mixed." From the newspaper *Russkii Invalid* came some qualified admiration, but other reviewers were critical of the amount of French used or were irritated that the novel (as it was so considered) did not have a real hero; it was felt that the book tended to glorify conservative family life, and lacked the authenticity of the period.

Tolstoy tried to ignore them all. He was helped by a distraction at home: Tanya Behrs, his adoring, lively sister-in-law, had fallen in love with Sergei, his own brother. In fact, they were both deeply in love, a passion in whose grip a certain essential piece of information went unmentioned: Sergei had a Gypsy mistress who lived with him, he had three children by her, with another on the way. Happy, feverish wedding preparations went forward, oddly, under the shadow of this secret, when, just days before the ceremony, Sergei Tolstoy, in a moment of guilt, confessed, and all was over. Tanya fell dangerously ill. Sonya was terribly upset, for although she had sustained moments of jealousy over Tanya's absorption with her husband, she loved her sister, and in some part, needed her constant good spirits. Throughout this all-encompassing drama, Leo Tolstoy acted as mediator and continued to write.

The next two parts of the novel, which Tolstoy decided to publish himself and offer in book form, were completed and began to sell quite well. Sonya gave birth to a son, Ilya, in May of 1866, their third child. The work went on. In response to the reviewers, Tolstoy published a defense of his work called *A Few Words About War and Peace,* which never seemed to clarify much. Critics were still skeptical and found the book hard to deal with. Yet a growing audience was enthusiastic. *War and Peace* was on everyone's lips. Even Turgenev started to come around. After the fourth part was published, he wrote: "There are unendurable things in it and there are wonderful things in it, and the wonderful things—they predominate—are so magnificently good that no one has ever written better and it is doubtful if anything as good has ever been written before."[16]

At the heart of Tolstoy's masterpiece is the expression of the heroic transformation of the Russian people, from their military losses of 1805 to the historic victory over Napoleon in 1812. Tolstoy's dislike of Europe can be felt in his creation of the character of the arrogant Napoleon. We learn from *War and Peace,* in the person and judgment of General Kutuzov, of Russian fatalism and endurance. We follow the kind and bumbling Pierre, the "natural" Russian, searching for the meaning of it all, and Prince Andrei, the embodiment of self-control and strength of will. We feel we are part of the process of life itself, allowed to participate in the central problems of human existence.

If General Kutuzov represents the quiet, heroic center of the book, then Natasha represents the life force; her vitality and spontaneity and altruism guarantee that life will go on. In the final chapters we find Natasha in her domestic realignment, married to Pierre, returned to a kind of pattern of family happiness. As it must be. "It is a terrible thing," Tolstoy observed, "when characters in a story do what is not in their nature to do." In *War and Peace,* destinies are fulfilled. History and nature are joined.

This sense of union, as well as the time frame of *War and Peace,* surely had its roots at Yasnaya Polyana. For at home, as Tolstoy sat writing at his desk, history and nature seemed joined there, at that time as well, and it may have lent strength to this most central theme of *War and Peace.* The setting of *War and Peace* combined with the history of his family and with nature, the simple forces of life, came together for him right at that point, on the estate which shaped his vision. It was here where his grandfather retired from his duties to the Crown and sat, under that window, listening to the serf orchestra, and it was here, on this same land, that Tolstoy now ploughed the fields and planted his birch trees. Destinies fulfilled. In 1865 he wrote to Alexandra Tolstoy, "It's now late autumn; the hunting which takes up a lot of my time has finished, and I'm writing a lot."[17] Could such harmony last?

After the sixth and final volume was published in 1869, the critical reception finally seemed to turn. "What mass and balance! No other literature offers us anything comparable," wrote the critic N. N. Strakhov in *The Dawn.* "Thousands of characters, thousands of scenes, the worlds of government and family, history and war, every moment of human life from the first mew of a newborn babe to the last gush of human life of the dying patriarch."

The critic Pogodin wrote to Tolstoy, "I melt, I weep, I rejoice."[18]

*　　*　　*

Did he rejoice? Did the man who worked for six years to produce what was (at last) regarded as a masterpiece, allow himself to rejoice? Well, yes and no. It seems that he did know what he had done. This non-novel, written on a grand scale, which energized a reading public, incited patriotism—indeed caused Tolstoy to be compared to Homer. That was fine with him. As well, he was moved by some of the favorable critics, most particularly N. N. Strakhov. True, he was a writer who cared nothing for literary life; yet, when the sun of literary achievement focused on him he must have felt its warmth. And since he had undertaken the publication of the last four volumes himself, at his own expense, and the book was so very much in demand, *War and Peace* was earning him money, which pleased Sonya.

What really happened right after *War and Peace* is that he collapsed with influenza. Through most of the winter of 1869–70 he lay in bed at Yasnaya Polyana, reading Schopenhauer, fighting inertia. He had felt an intimate identification with the main characters of *War and Peace,* for they each represented part of him. When the writing of the book was over he felt an understandable yet terrible emptiness. Of course he had plans and tasks—he would learn Greek, or maybe write a play, or learn to ride a bicycle as his friend Fet had done. He ice-skated, amusing those around him with his figure eights. He hunted. Yet one senses in his correspondence a certain lassitude. To Fet, February 4, 1870: "I received your letter, dear Afansy Afanasyevitch, on the 1st of February, but even had I received it somewhat sooner I could not have come. You write, 'I am alone, alone!.' And when I read it I thought, What a lucky fellow—alone! I have a wife, three children and a fourth at the breast, two old aunts, a nurse, and two housemaids. And they are all ill together: fever, high temperature, weakness, headaches, and coughs. In that state your letter found me. They are now beginning to get better but out of ten people, I and my old aunt alone turn up at the dinner table. And since yesterday I myself am ill with my chest and side. There is much, very much to tell you about. I have been reading a lot of Shakespeare, Goethe, Pushkin, Gogol and Molière, and about all of them there is much I want to say to you. I do not take in a single magazine or newspaper this year, and I consider it very useful not to."[19]

Despite this quite bleak description, the life of Yasnaya Polyana renewed itself with the advent of spring. An English governess was hired to deal with the earthy, country-bred Tolstoy children, and Sonya now went about the house holding an English dictionary. The apple orchards were in full bloom,

The first four Tolstoy children, photographed in 1863. Left to right: Ilya, Lev, Tatyana, and Sergei.

in the evenings everyone gathered for family games. Tanya had married her rather dull cousin, Sasha Kuzminsky, but remained at the center of all fun. Croquet games were played after dinner, often by candlelight. Sonya produced two more children—another son, Lev, and in 1871 a daughter, (Masha), who would eventually become her father's favorite. It was a time of abundance and productivity. A cousin recalls: "We lived gaily, lightheartedly and youthfully, then."[20]

Tolstoy remained restless. Questions of religion and universal truth dogged him more than ever. How should one live? Is there nothing left after death but a bit of earth over which grass will grow? The years spent writing the masterpiece had offered him both distraction and opportunity. Working on *War and Peace* had permitted him to invest in his characters the sweeping sympathy that he often lacked for those around him; perhaps he suspected that through his fiction he lived more fully. Now that the epic work was over, he turned his eternal questions in on himself. What is the purpose of life on earth? What is justice? He searched within his reading. He scribbled in his notebook.

Family members and household servants in the process of making jam, just outside the main house.

Sonya noted his melancholy and hoped that the start of another novel might bring back his good humor. It was not to be. At least not for a while.

The success of *War and Peace* had brought him some extra money. Tolstoy decided to buy some more property—an estate in a nearby province was advertised. Why not go and look at it? En route, an extraordinary event took place, one which plunged him into despair, perhaps into a temporary madness.

Accompanied by one servant, he took the long train ride north, then hired a coach. At dusk he stopped for the night at an inn in the town of Arzamas. Tolstoy slept in a plain square room, yet the whole atmosphere of the inn gave him a sharp sense of foreboding. At around two in the morning he awoke with an agonizing terror. Something in the room was tormenting him. From his later story, *Memoirs of a Madman,* he tells us what it was:

> I said to myself, Why am I depressed? What am I afraid of?
> "Me!" answered the voice of Death. "I am here!"

A cold shudder ran down my back. Yes! Death! It will come—it is here—and it ought not to be. Had I actually been facing death I could not have suffered as much as I did then. Then I should have been frightened. But now I was not frightened. I saw and felt the approach of death, and at the same time I felt that such a thing ought not to exist.

My whole being was conscious of the necessity and the right to live, and yet I felt that Death was being accomplished.

Death. Terror. Anguish. He refers later to "the tearing within that could not be torn apart." He began to pray. He felt that death was taking him over, he could feel it entering his skin, ripping at his organs, silencing his brain. In a blind panic he woke his servant and ordered that the horses be readied—they must leave at once. He then collapsed and fell into an undisturbed sleep.

The next morning, Tolstoy made a cursory trip to look at the property, then tore back to the safety of Yasnaya Polyana. In this terrible night the shadow of death, which had hovered in his childhood, had presented itself again. But it was the depth of his despair which terrified him.

"I cannot sufficiently describe the joyous and happy frame of mind that usually reigned at Yasnaya Polyana," wrote Stepan Behrs, Tolstoy's brother-in-law. "Its source was always Lev Nikolayevich. In conversation about abstract questions, about the education of children, about outside matters—his opinion was always the most interesting. When playing croquet, or during walks, he enlivened us all by his humor . . . He himself did not take part in the mushroom hunts, much in vogue at Yasnaya, but he knew how to encourage us to do so."[21]

It is doubtful that Stepan Behrs remembered or was aware of two earlier observations by Sonya: "I cannot see it but I can sense his indifference to life which began last winter . . . He says that it is old age." And she records that he "feels a terrible burden; that it is all over for him and that it is time for him to die and be gone."[22]

But by Behrs's account, we see Tolstoy enjoying the best of humor, which suggests again the split in temperament, the ability to recover quickly from a dark period, with a "joyous and happy frame of mind," while still feeling the rumblings of despair, given extra poignancy since the night at Arzamas.

Tolstoy, photographed as War and Peace *and* Anna Karenina *were completed and established as masterpieces.*

Stepan Behrs continues: "With me, he liked to mow or to use the rake; to do gymnastics, to race, and occasionally to play leap frog. Though far inferior to him in strength, for he could lift 180 lbs with one hand, I could easily match him in a race, but seldom passed him for I was always laughing. That mood accompanied all our exercises. Whenever we happened to pass when mowers were at work, he would go up to them and borrow a scythe from the one who seemed the most tired. I of course imitated his example. He would then ask me, why we, with well-developed muscles, cannot mow six days on end, though a peasant does it on rye bread, and sleeping on the damp earth. 'You just try it under such conditions,' he would add in conclusion."[23]

Though the peasants were no longer in bondage, carrying the empire on their backs, as was often the description, the emancipation of 1861 did little to change the poverty or the restrictions of their lives. (Most received an allotment of land, approximately eight acres per head of household, and were paid in goods or in days of unpaid labor for the master.) But it was the same misery—rye bread and underheated wood huts. From his earliest years, Tolstoy had always identified profoundly with the peasants. It is not clear that he knew exactly what it meant to be a peasant, but he was anguished by the knowledge that he lived by their labor. He knew the ways in which they suffered. Remember the boy who cried when the stable boy was beaten? As an adult landowner, Tolstoy championed the peasant cause. Named Arbiter of the Peace in 1861, a kind of grievance board of Tula county, he decided consistently in favor of the peasant. He was one arbiter the surrounding landowners would never forget.

In his later years, Tolstoy envied what he felt to be the peasants' innate wisdom and simplicity of nature, their clear acceptance of human destiny. Platon Karatayev, the round muzhik whom we see on the battlefield in *War and Peace,* is held up by Tolstoy for us all to understand and admire.

Yet for Tolstoy, who tended to take things to greater dimensions, there was more: He wished to live like the peasant and thus purify himself. He wanted to capture for himself the utter naturalness of the peasant soul. In earlier conversations with his young students at his school, as he sat on the porch at night, he talked of this. Understandably, they thought he was joking. He was not.

The problem was, he couldn't live the life of the peasant. The aristocrat could not be made over, and he knew it. But how often he thought about it! The world of the peasants was one of the dominance of heart over head, of purity over artifice. The muzhik knows how to die, he often said.

And he knew he did not.

4

ANNA KARENINA AND *A CONFESSION*
[1869-1880]

The question now became, what could follow *War and Peace?* In December of 1872, Sonya wrote, "Lyovochka is still reading historical books of the time of Peter the Great and is much interested in them, he notes down all the characters of various people, their traits as well as the way of life of the boyars [gentry] and the peasants and Peter's activity. He does not yet know what will come of it all but it seems to me that we shall have another prose poem like *War and Peace.*"[1]

Why not a novel on the subject of Peter the Great? He was surely grand enough. Oddly, the powerful figure of Peter, the tsar who transformed Russia, did not really *stir* Tolstoy. Peter the Great was too Western, for one thing. Despite considerable research on Peter and some early chapters, the question still remained unanswered. What could follow *War and Peace?*

During this time the Tolstoys' daughter Masha was born, their fifth child. Expansion on the main house became necessary, for not only was the family burgeoning but Tolstoy had decided to reopen the peasant school—the little school, which he could call into play with a wave of the hand, again proved a kind of refuge for him. Since the former schoolhouse, the other wing of the old house, was now occupied by the bailiff,* Alexei Stepanovitsh, it was

* Overseer of the estate.

Sonya's bedroom.

decided that the children should all come to the main house. And to add an extra stimulant, Tolstoy gave himself a new project—this time he would accompany his teaching with a series of perfect children's textbooks, which he would write. He called them Primers. There were four in all.

The Primers, also called ABC Books, contained some vivid autobiographical stories, translations of Aesop's fables, chapters on natural science, selections from Lives of the Saints, and a lengthy section on arithmetic; the last subject Tolstoy sought to explain in his own way, ignoring conventional methods. Again, peasant children bundled in sheepskin coats gathered on cold winter mornings. Sonya, after morning lessons with her own children, joined in the teaching, as did the older Tolstoy children—Sergei, who was eight, and Tatyana, who was seven.

To accommodate this beehive of activity, a splendid two-story addition was constructed onto the house in 1871. A new entrance hall, and above, on the second floor, an enlarged dining room with parquet floors. Tolstoy's study was moved from the vaulted-ceiling room where he had written *War and Peace* to the new part of the house—a lovely room on the main floor with a niche in the wall where a bust of his brother Nikolai was mounted. Bookshelves

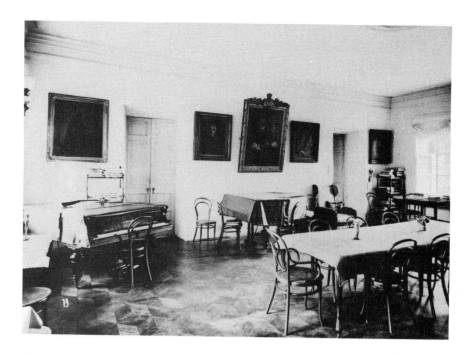

The zala photographed from the parlor. Note the two pianos.

divided the room, and they were supported by huge cross beams. To celebrate the finish of this new section of the house, a masquerade ball was given, in which Tolstoy regaled everyone by appearing as a goat.

And from the upstairs of the recently completed wing, a new sight appeared on the horizon: a distant view of the newly constructed Moscow–Kursk railroad line.

The railroad is no small player in the life or the novels of Leo Tolstoy. Before the reign of Alexander II, who built up the railroad system, goods were hauled from the northern provinces, painfully and slowly, by dogs, horses, or reindeer, and in the south by oxen and mule. For the most part people traveled by horse-drawn sledges, that is open sleighs on runners (and without springs!). In the winter, if lucky, one could make good time on snow-packed roads, although they were only sketchily marked with posts. In this coldest of seasons a sledge could race along over frozen rivers, but most of the time travel was slow and uncomfortable. Roads were often all but impassable in the spring because of mud and permanently frozen subsoil. In 1857, when Leo Tolstoy took his first trip to Europe, there were 671 versts (447 miles) of working railroad. By 1876, the railroad had expanded to cover 16,700 versts. The railroad served to free Russia from its own bondage.

Tolstoy, reacting predictably to the world of "progress," considered the railroad to be an affliction, like the telegraph, a corrupting European influence. He wrote: "Which . . . benefits does the railroad bring the people? It increases temptations; it destroys the woods; it draws people from their labors; it raises the price of grain."[2] He added, somewhat presumptuously, that the peasants were "hostile to the railroad." His contempt in this case was no match for the zeal of the tsar, who laid thirteen thousand versts of track throughout his reign.

Despite his sour attitude, Tolstoy did use the railroad; when he traveled with Sonya he rode first class, or third class when by himself, that he might be able to talk to the peasants. Apparently the motion of the train continually caused him "disagreeable sensations."[3]

On January 18, 1872, Sonya wrote to her sister Tanya: "We have had another dramatic incident here in Yasnaya. You remember Anna Stepanovna over at the Bibikovs? Well, she was jealous of all the governesses . . . and threw herself under a train and was crushed to death."[4]

Madness of all sorts was possible on these isolated estates; Bibikov was a neighboring landowner and Anna Stepanovna Pirogova was his mistress. When Tolstoy heard this news he went immediately to the inquest at the station in Tula; her mangled body lay in the engine house, skull bone exposed. Tolstoy had known Bibikov and his family. The circumstances of the woman who threw herself under the train seized his imagination. Peter the Great was dismissed. Anna Karenina was born.

The second great novel was achieved in a markedly different manner from that of *War and Peace*. A necessary period of gestation followed the Bibikov affair, during which Tolstoy considered the structure of the new novel. For some months he had been thinking of writing a story about a woman disgraced by sexual scandal, an idea made vivid by his married sister, Marya, who had run off with a Swedish nobleman and endured a long period of social ostracism. In March of 1873, Tolstoy happened to read the first line of a Pushkin novel which intrigued him: "The guests had arrived at the country house." This sentence, which he thought served to take the reader right into the heart of the story, released a demon in him which allowed him to plunge immediately into the heart of *Anna Karenina*. (The opening of *Anna Karenina* is heralded by a

Study where Anna Karenina *was written.*

far more memorable first sentence: "All happy families are alike but an un-happy family is unhappy after its own fashion.") He began writing with excitement, even elation, and finished a first draft in a few weeks' time, if this letter to Strakhov in May of 1873 can be believed: "I'm writing a novel which has no connection to Peter the First. I've been writing it for more than a month now and have finished it in first draft form. This novel—I mean a novel, the first in my life—is very dear to my heart and I'm quite absorbed by it, but in spite of that, philosophic problems have been occupying me very much this spring. In the letter which I didn't send to you I wrote about this novel and about how it came to me unwittingly, thanks to the divine Pushkin whom I happened to pick up . . ."[5]

The divine Pushkin perhaps, but in truth it was a divine Anna who drove the novel into being. In an early version of the book he had molded Anna into a rather plain creature, but soon he redrew her physical being into the beauty and power that made Anna, without doubt, the favorite heroine of Russian fiction. He too was enchanted, perhaps even a little afraid of her. Anna, restless and "intoxicated with life," and Tolstoy, restless and intoxicated with life—were they not one?

In the midst of the splendid panorama of nineteenth-century Russian society, Anna falls in love with the polished and persistent Captain Vronsky and abandons her husband and son. The restrictive forces of society are pitted against redemptive sexual passion, the order of accepted family life contested by the power of love. Anna is ruled by her heart. Tolstoy searches out her passions and variations, her final torment. For a man who had some very old-fashioned ideas about women, it was remarkable that he seemed to release himself to write one of the most profoundly psychological studies of a woman in the history of literature. Anna Karenina is life itself; passion has at its core both life and death. Anna's death, as she throws herself under the engine at the railroad station, is played out with dread and foreboding. Tolstoy, in his relentless search for truth, does not ask that the readers judge Anna, he only asks that we feel life in its shifting patterns, its many manifestations. The "seer of the flesh," as he was called, gave us a book with great scenes—the horse race, the meeting between Anna and Vronsky in the railroad car—scenes and characters with whom an entire country could feel a personal identification.

And Anna is but half the equation. In this novel of pairs and internal linkage, we see her counterpart in the character of Konstantine Levin, the country landowner. He is perhaps the closest representative of Tolstoy himself. Through Levin, Tolstoy confronts questions of Christianity, the artifice of society, the value of the life of the peasantry, the sanctity of marriage. And we feel life as Levin feels it, at close range. Simply, with nature's sensuality and warmth etched in perfect detail: "The longer Levin mowed, the oftener he experienced those moments of oblivion when it was not his arms which swung the scythe but the scythe seemed to mow of itself, a body full of life and consciousness of its own, and as though by magic, without a thought being given to it, the work did itself regularly and carefully. These were the most blessed moments."[6] Only a man who has ploughed the field himself could render such moments.

Yet Tolstoy the writer could never content himself with the purely aesthetic outlook, for it was the central problems of human existence that plagued and compelled him. He poured his concerns into the character of Levin: "All that day, while talking to the bailiff and the peasants, at home with his wife, with Dolly, her children, and his father-in-law, Levin's thoughts were busy with the one and only subject, outside his farming, that interested him at this time, and in everything he sought a bearing on his questions: What am I? Where am I? And why am I here?"[7]

And who is it that provides an answer, or a partial answer, at least? Fiodr, a peasant working in the barn. Live for your soul, he tells Levin, and do not forget God.

"A novel joyous feeling enveloped Levin. At the peasant's words . . . dim but important thoughts crowded into his mind, as if they had broken loose from some place where they had been locked up, and all rushing forward toward one goal, whirled in his head, blinding him with their light."

Would an explanation so simple suffice for Tolstoy himself?

If Levin finds some answers and can go on with his life, Anna does not. Mired in her own tragedy, Anna throws herself under the wheels of an oncoming train.

While Tolstoy wrote the first sections in a kind of passionate frenzy, Sonya copied the manuscript. Much of it must have given her pleasure, for the courtship and marriage of Levin and Kitty Shtcherbatsky, so warmly rendered, closely resembled her own. Was he reconfirming his love for her, through these passages? She copied these luminous passages late into the night.

Sonya was often bored with the endless winter evenings, where not a sound could be heard but the occasional cracking of the birch trees. From time to time she felt genuine ennui, a longing for Moscow, for the bustle of society. Yet she was no listless figure from *Three Sisters,* waiting passively for something to happen. Sonya was well aware of her position as the wife of a literary genius, and everything about life with Tolstoy the writer thrilled her. It was his moods of religious inquiry and morbid scholarship which gave her concern. She had very much wanted him to find his next masterpiece; *Anna Karenina* had arrived just in time.

Now, as she tried to decipher his crabbed handwriting, she felt the return to the reasonable, rhythmic life they had enjoyed during the working of *War and Peace.* Her household was extraordinarily full. While bearing babies almost constantly (a son, Petya, was born in June of 1872), she instructed the older children in French, taught them to read and write, made most of their clothes by hand, and dealt with a fleet of servants. One hesitates before characterizing life at Yasnaya Polyana as on *even keel,* and yet, for this brief time, during the beginning of *Anna Karenina,* such a description might apply.

Leo Tolstoy had a daily routine in which his principal passions—writing and hunting—were juggled but rarely bypassed. He rose at about nine o'clock, dressed and had tea, then headed down toward his study, where he would stop, his son Ilya recalls, at the doorway of the zala, ". . . and remain rooted to the same spot for as much as a half hour, quite unaware that his tea was getting cold, and talk and talk; and somehow it was always just then that the discussion grew most animated and interesting." In his *Reminiscences,* Ilya remembers:

> We all knew this spot by the door so well, and knew for certain that when Papa reached it, with his tumbler full of tea in his hand, he was sure to stop there with the intention of clinching the argument in a word or two . . . At last he would go off to his work, and we all dispersed, in winter to the different schoolrooms, in summer to the croquet lawn or somewhere about the garden; my mother settled down in the zala to make clothes for the babies or to copy out something she had not got finished overnight; and till three or four in the afternoon silence reigned in the house.
>
> Then my father came out of his study and went off for his afternoon exercise. Sometimes he took a dog and his gun with him, sometimes he rode . . .[8]

A modern writer would be more than pleased with such a schedule—harmony, of sorts, balance, the world of children and dogs, the resplendent countryside; despite his philosophic concerns, the side of his complex character which was intoxicated with life still had the upper hand. The moralist was in the wings.

Into this period of relative tranquillity appeared, once again, ever and oppressive, the specter of death. The baby Petya died in the winter of 1873, and Tanya Kuminskaya's five-year-old daughter, of whom Tolstoy was particularly fond, died in the same year. In 1874, the fragile and sainted Aunt Toinette—and there was no dearer figure in Tolstoy's life—closed her eyes. Sonya gave birth to a son, Nikolai, who died of meningitis in a few short months. Aunt Toinette's room in the house had been taken by the far less agreeable but nonetheless commanding figure of Aunt Pelageya, who died in a complicated manner a few months later. As if this succession of ghastly deaths was not enough, months later Sonya gave birth to a daughter, Varvara, who lived only one day. Coffins, large and small, were brought to the house. Priests, hymns, the smell of incense in the common rooms, "fear, horror, death . . . special foods, agitation, doctors—it was torture," Tolstoy wrote Fet.[9]

The presentiment of death is never far from the center of Russian life. Death as a part of life, contained in the folklore, a constant theme in literature, the acceptance of death among the peasantry—yet even with this preparation, the accumulated toll on the Tolstoy household was dreadful. They had suffered six deaths in two years.

Nonetheless, the first installments of *Anna Karenina* were finished and published in late 1875. But the exhilaration of the early, more productive months had been broken. "My God, if only someone would finish *Anna Karenina* for me!" Tolstoy wrote. "It's unbearably repulsive!"[10] The work on *Anna* was abandoned for long periods of time, particularly in the summer, when the whole family packed up and went to Samara. What relief the chalky and spare landscape provided, with the hypnotic warmth of the Bashkirs, their magnificent horses, the medicinal effects of the mare's milk. In 1870 Tolstoy had bought a huge tract of land in the Buzuluk section of Samara, and now it gave the family distraction. And time off from the "tiresome, boring *Anna*."

Had he turned against *Anna*? Well, it's not quite clear why he referred to his heroine, whom he surely loved, with such disdain. On his return to Yasnaya that summer of 1875 he wrote on August 25: "Now I'm settling down again to dull, commonplace *Anna Karenina* and I pray to God just to give me the strength to get it off my hands as quickly as possible."[11] Questions of the spirit were preoccupying him and yet the novel was of him, the characters drawn from his own psyche, and they demanded his sweat and blood.

By the next spring he wrote to Strakhov: "I'm disgusted with what I've written, and now there are proofs for the April issue and I'm afraid I shan't have the strength to correct them. Everything in them is bad, everything needs to be revised and revised—everything that's been printed—and I need to cross it all out and disown . . ."[12]

On and on, wringing his hands—and one might well ask why. Tolstoy did tend to considerable exaggeration; he once referred to a fine short story of his as "an abomination." But now his dark moods had returned, and he was both preoccupied with religious concerns and increasingly uncomfortable with his world. His letters to both Alexandra ("You say you don't know what I believe in. Strange and terrible to say . . .") and Strakhov ("dear Nikolay

Nikolayevich, I had just replied to your philosophic letter when I got your heartening reply to mine . . .") suggest intense and passionate exchanges, that he is entering a renewed period of wrestling with himself.

By spring of 1877, the last sequences of *Anna Karenina* were finished and run in *Russkii Vestnik*. This monthly publication, often described as a fat journal, had now published all of *Anna* except the very last section, dropped after a squabble with the editor, Katkov. The critics received the novel—and it surely was a novel this time—with enthusiasm. And in "society," everyone went wild. Compared with *War and Peace, Anna Karenina* is a work of some pessimism, yet Moscow and St. Petersburg devoured it. Cousin Alexandra wrote: "Every chapter has society rearing up on its hind legs, and there is no end to the commenting and praise and gossip and argument, as though it were something that had affected every individual personally."[13]

N. N. Strakhov, the critic who had by this time become something of an insider in Tolstoy's world, reported the almost unanimous, rapturous praise for *Anna Karenina*: "Everyone is dumb with admiration of the February issue . . . Now there is a roar of satisfaction; it is as if you are throwing food out to starving men . . . it is incredible how many people are reading it." Dostoyevsky, according to Strakhov, was "waving his arms about and calling you a god of art." In a calmer moment, in his *Diary of a Writer,* Dostoyevsky suggested: "Anna Karenina is a perfect work of art, appearing at exactly the right moment, utterly unlike anything that is being published in Europe; its theme is totally Russian."[14]

And how did this extraordinary praise sit with Tolstoy? His daughter Alexandra, in her book *A Life of My Father,* suggests that he wished to avoid the corrupting influence of praise and burned the reviews that Strakhov sent without reading them. If one cannot quite believe this purifying gesture, his new bouts of spiritual fear and inner turmoil at this time cannot be doubted.

The Tolstoy family, led by Sonya, regularly observed the ceremonies of the Russian Orthodox church, including the many holidays and fasting at Lent; a priest came regularly to the house to hold vespers. Tolstoy, though at times cavalier with this ritual or that, participated. But during the final months of his struggle to complete *Anna Karenina,* in his doubts and search for the direction his life was to take, Tolstoy turned to religious ritual with additional fervor. He also spent hours reading the Gospels and Renan's *Vie de Jésus.* His preoccupation was felt throughout the household. "As my Father grew more religious," Ilya Tolstoy recalls, "so did we."

But it was relatively short-lived. The search for truth had established in Tolstoy a lifetime habit of remorseless questioning. The more he sought answers by immersion in religious rites, the more doubtful, or perhaps the more repelled by it all, he became. "I attended services, knelt morning and evening in prayer, fasted and prepared to receive the Eucharist . . . but nearly two-thirds of the whole service either remained quite incomprehensible, or, when I forced an explanation into them, made me feel that I was lying, and thereby quite destroying my relation to God and losing all possibility of believing."[15]

A year later, as soon as *Anna Karenina* was off his hands, Tolstoy hastened to the Optina Monastery, where he sought an audience with a famous elder, Father Ambrose. Although no one quite knows why, he came back greatly dissatisfied. Ilya Tolstoy remembers the feeling that "Father had changed and something was happening to him . . . He began to criticize the rites and traditions of the Church."[16]

Years earlier, when stationed in the Crimea, Tolstoy had declared somewhat grandly, though sincerely, that he wished to establish a new Christianity, a religion free of dogma and ritual. Now his need for faith tormented him, and the further he investigated formal religions the more reasonable his earlier declaration seemed.

He closed himself in his study for days on end. "At this time, the following happened to me: In the course of a whole year, almost every minute I asked myself whether I had not better kill myself with a rope or a bullet. And at the same time as I was experiencing the thought and observations I have described, my heart was agonized by a tormenting feeling. I can only describe this feeling as a quest for God."[17] He felt like a man tossing about in a boat, who looks back, only to discover a new direction he should be taking. To reach the shore, he must struggle against the current. Thus Tolstoy's spiritual crisis was brought on by the feeling of loss of solid ground beneath his feet, heightened by the sharp awareness of the schism between the demands of the church and his own reason and conscience. And it hit him with full fury.

A Confession, begun during this dark period, is a remarkable work, in which he rationally and precisely traces his own life and thinking surrounding the spiritual crisis. Though Tolstoy somewhat exaggerates the debauchery of his early years, *A Confession* remains one of the most well-reasoned documents ever written. In an additional and important clue to the nature of his crisis, he records: "The life of our circle of society, the rich, the learned, not only repelled me, but lost all meaning."[18]

If life had lost all meaning, then were not his achievements worthless?

Consider for a moment where Lev Nikolayevich Tolstoy stood in the world: He was fifty-one years old, he owned a vast and abundant estate, he came of distinguished ancestry, and his own distinction had already surpassed that of his forebears. He had written two of the greatest novels in literature, he had plenty of money, spoke six languages, and had at his hand the pleasures of the hunt and the richness of nature. He had created schools on his own property and championed the cause of the peasantry, who loved him. He had an accomplished wife whom he loved and seven children. He even played a good piano.

But if life had lost all meaning, what lay in front of him? Did not the rope that could easily be thrown up over the cross beams in his study then seem a reasonable solution? Tolstoy was a rational man, an empiricist, and philosophy and science had offered him no answers. He found in the formal established church nothing but swollen hypocrisy and a distortion of Christ's teachings.

But at last there was a little light.

By poring through the Gospels, he found some truths to cling to. From the Sermon on the Mount he came upon a cornerstone of faith that he could accept. Perhaps he might even rejoice, for he managed to isolate five commandments which seemed to express the essence of Christ's teaching and provide a sufficient guide to a nobler life on earth. And it was, was it not, a new and nobler life that he wanted for himself and for others? Loosely rephrased, here were his chosen commandments: (1) Avoid anger against your brother, (2) Avoid lust, (3) Do not swear, nor take binding oaths, (4) Do not resist evil, use no physical violence, and (5) Love your enemies.

At last, he could give meaning to his rejection of the mystical in religious life, for he had discovered a kind of daily Christianity. He would try living a spiritual life outside the Church. Salvation—giving meaning to life—could be achieved by earthly virtue. "Every day to think of God, of one's soul, and therefore to set the love of one's neighbor above mere bestial existence," he wrote. Brotherly love. Earthly virtue. Earthly happiness? Of course. And, a voice told him, he would not be without God if he could live *seeking* God.

So it would be. He would live simply, seeking God. In the next months he began to take long walks on the old Moscow–Kiev road which ran near Yasnaya Polyana. Here he could talk to pilgrims, simple itinerants, travelers moving from one holy place to another. He wanted to renew his feeling for the folk language; he wanted to rediscover old Russia. He heard wonderful tales, shared the pilgrims' prayers, shared their suppers.

Did not the peasants and the wandering pilgrims possess the honest Christianity and simple faith he sought? Hadn't they always?

News traveled slowly in rural Russia. Ilya remembers this:

> On the first of March, Papa, as usual, went for a walk along the highway before dinner. After the heavy rains of winter a thaw had set in. There were already deep ruts in the roads and the hollows were filled with water. Because of the bad weather we had not sent in to Tula and there were no newspapers.
>
> On the highway Papa met some kind of wandering Italian with a barrel organ and a fortune-telling bird. He was coming on foot from the direction of Tula. They fell into conversation— "Where from? Where to?"
>
> "From Tula, bad business, I had not food, my bird has not eaten, they killed the Tsar."
>
> "What Tsar? Who killed him? When?"
>
> "The Russian Tsar, St. Petersburg, threw a bomb, we got the papers."
>
> When he came home Papa immediately told us about the death of Alexander II, and the newspapers which arrived the next day confirmed the news, giving precise details. I remember the depressing effect on Father of this senseless murder.[19]

The revolutionary People's Will party had begun to step up its terrorist attacks. The murder of the "Liberator Tsar" brought to the throne a harsher, more autocratic figure, Alexander III. From Yasnaya Polyana, Tolstoy wrote him an impassioned letter asking for clemency for the killers, *out of Christian love*. The assassins were swiftly executed. Tolstoy's plea was considered a lone voice in the wilderness.

In the year of the accession of Tsar Alexander III, 1881, a new Tolstoy son was born, Alexis. Another son, Andrei, then age four, was sickly, and Sonya ministered to him day and night. Eight children now filled the rooms of Yasnaya Polyana.

"I don't care for children until they are two or three years old," wrote Tolstoy in a sweeping manner. "I don't understand them. There are two types of men; hunters and nonhunters. Nonhunters love babies and can pick them up and hold them in their arms; hunters are terrified, sickened and filled with pity at the sight of a baby." He added, "I know of no exception to that rule."[20]

His children adored him. If he "didn't care for children until they were three," he took a passionate interest in their education and their physical development as they grew. Tatyana and little Masha worshiped him. He taught them to ride, took them all bathing in the Voronka River. And of course the boys joined him in the hunt.

Coursing, hunting for hares with the dogs, was a favorite activity for the twelve-year-old Ilya:

"The excitement began the night before," he remembers. "Would the weather settle? Would the snow stop in the night? Or would there be a blizzard?

"Early in the morning we ran out half dressed into the zala and examined the horizon. If the line of the horizon was clearly defined, that meant that the weather was settled and we could go. But if the horizon melted into the sky, that meant the snow was drifting in the open and the tracks made at night were covered over. We waited for Papa or sometimes summoned courage to send to wake him; and at last we were all ready and started out.

"This sort of hunting is particularly interesting because, by the tracks of the hare, you can trace out the whole of his nocturnal life . . . When you came on his track you had to raise your hand with the hunting crop in it and give a long, mysterious whistle. Then the rest of the hunters rode up, Papa went forward along the track to disengage it, and, holding our breath with excitement, we crept on behind him. Once we ran down twelve grey hares and two foxes in the new snow in a single day."[21]

How easy it is to imagine the endless fields of snow, a hazy uncertain horizon, children sitting by frosted windows—and then Tolstoy, as Papa, the instigator of pleasure, announces that the next morning they will go out coursing! Did it not make the long winter bearable? For him? For them? And what binding, constant, and exhilarating pleasure!

Then why did he give it up?

"I can't remember exactly when my Father gave up hunting," Ilya writes. "I think it was in the middle eighties, about the time he became a vegetarian."

For Tolstoy to abandon hunting was to sacrifice an abiding passion. Yet in concert with his new godly life, he vowed to give up worldly pleasures, which consisted of a great deal, in his case. "To save his soul," he wrote in *A Confession,* "a man must live Godly, and to live Godly, he must renounce all the pleasures of life." (Perhaps renouncing gave him pleasure of a different sort.) He would sacrifice meat, tobacco (and he loved to smoke), reinvest himself in manual labor, yes, give up the hunt, that he might live and proclaim a new Christianity. The question really was, Could he do it? The question throughout his life remained, Could he reconcile his life with his beliefs?

Tolstoy's spiritual crisis was slow to be understood in the bustling household of Yasnaya Polyana. Ongoing daily life, lessons, teatimes abundant with tarts and pirozhki, joyous Christmas parties—these happy traditions were firmly planted and, one might say, necessary for survival in the splendid isolation of Yasnaya Polyana.

Through most of the children's early years, in the evenings after tea, around eight, everyone gathered in the zala. Often Tolstoy played the piano

Everyone gathered in the evening in the "Serious Talk" corner: M. A. Stakovich, Tolstoy, Tatyana, Masha Kuzminskaya (Sonya's niece), Masha Tolstoy, Sonya. Sitting atop the folding screen, Misha behind Andrei.

Household servants.

or read aloud. "The best hours of the day," Ilya called it. In one side of the zala, the serious talk took place; across the way on the floor, the children played games, made drawings, or just listened. Everyone felt bound together in the long winter nights and the comforts of physical nearness and shared blood. The life of the multiplying and exuberant family, with five tutors and nine house servants, moved of its own force.

In later biographies, the Tolstoy children suggest that they recognized a feeling of isolation on the part of their father at around this time but did not give it the properties of inner reconstruction that were in fact the case. His oldest daughter, Tatyana, writes, "Shortly before 1880 all my father's aspirations became diverted to new goals. It was a process which began almost imperceptibly."[22]

In 1882 he was certainly well able to share, or perhaps even create, utter merriment. Tatyana: "I was lying down in Ilya's room with a frightful pain, Ilya groaning too from fever, when all at once in came Papa, and asked how we were, and said, 'It's even funny,' and suddenly there we were, all three, roaring with laughter, so that Papa had to sit down, and nearly fell off his chair onto the floor, he roared so. I cannot remember ever laughing so much; nor can Ilya."[23]

View of the Voronka River, which runs through the estate, and the bathing hut that Tolstoy and his family used often.

Laughter, laughter. Yes, it was everywhere, and in games with the children, he became one of them. An absolute favorite game was called Numidian Cavalry. Tolstoy, as the presumed leader of the cavalry, would charge throughout the house at a gallop as the screaming children fell into step behind him. This game came in particularly handy as an antidote to lengthy visits from dull neighbors. And while playing the piano, which he loved, if Tolstoy missed a note or lapsed into confusion, he would rise, fling off a boot, announce to the forgathered that the boot was responsible, that now things would be better, and return to the keyboard. Although he tended to be huffy about the children having too many toys, he bought most of them himself on trips to Tula or Moscow.

Ilya: "Papa almost never punishes us. But if he looks me straight in the eye, he knows everything I'm thinking and I get uneasy. I can lie to Mamma, but not to Papa. He knows all our secrets."[24] But they, as yet, did not know his.

And what of Sonya? The process of change in Tolstoy which Tatyana describes as *imperceptible* was quite perceptible to her. She wrote her sister:

Tolstoy, photographed in Moscow in 1885.

"Lyovachka is always at work, as he expresses it; but alas! he is writing some sort of religious discussion. He reads and reads till his head aches, and all to show how incompatible the Church is with the teaching of the Gospel. Hardly ten people in Russia will be interested in it; but there is nothing to be done. I only wish that he would get it done quicker, that it would pass like an illness."[25]

Sonya was wrong. Millions in Russia and the world over became interested, and it was not to pass. Tolstoy's self-imposed internal emigration at Yasnaya Polyana was over. He was on a new road.

5

A SOUL DIVIDED
[1880-1890]

In the zala, the largest and most beautiful of the second-floor rooms at Yasnaya Polyana, portraits of the Tolstoy and Volkonsky ancestors line the walls. None is more imposing than that of Count Ilya Andreyevich, Tolstoy's paternal grandfather.

One can but imagine what Count Ilya might have thought as he looked down from his perch on the wall. It is August of 1881, and Countess Tolstoy, her sister, and their children scurry through the halls and closets preparing an evening theatrical. General hilarity and a great deal of noise fill the air. An elaborate dinner is in the works. Count Ilya is pleased. This is the way he lived life; this is the way it should be.

In his study Leo Tolstoy sits surrounded by the Gospels and religious writing, in a mood of deep contemplation. He is searching out answers to the great questions, and the noise from the zala annoys him. Count Ilya Andreyevich is puzzled. Why such solitude, such anguish over the fate of one's soul?

Count Ilya Andreyevich once served as governor-general of the province of Kazan, an important post, and he carried out his duties with such lavish attention to entertaining that he was eventually removed from the job. Apparently he could refuse no request, and restraint was a word that never occurred to him. Count Ilya gave parties that lasted three and four days. Serf theater, fanciful plays in which the serving class joined in the elaborate entertainment, had a strong tradition during much of the eighteenth century, and it flourished under his roof. The finest sturgeon was sent in from Astrakhan, and nothing but French wines would do. He even went so far as to have his bed sheets sent by train to Holland to be laundered, accompanied by two serfs. Nothing was out of reach for Count Ilya, who in addition to his extravagance was apparently of a kindly and happy disposition.

That his descendant, Count Lev Nikolayevich, dressed in simple tunic, now be burdened with the very fruits of the social structure that Count Ilya Andreyevich had lived with so easily—yes, he would be puzzled.

As well, and perhaps more importantly, Lev Nikolayevich had broken with the formal Church. Belief in the sanctity of the Russian Orthodox church was at the center of cultural and emotional life. No matter what the social standing, boyar or muzhik, everyone felt attachment to the rituals of the Church—the liturgy, communion, lighting of candles. Among the landed gentry, these rituals folded easily and naturally into the ebb and flow of their days. After a particularly riotous eight-hour dinner, resplendent with talk and music and entertainment, the force of habit called the merrymakers all to morning services, often held right on the estate, presided over by the local prelate. Everyone went.

That Tolstoy should have proclaimed his conversion away from this easy emotional outlet and toward a new religion, one based on reason and stern, earthly values, was an extraordinary, independent act. While accepting the teachings of Christ, he had denounced Christ's sanctity and divinity. As well, he felt that the Church had simply become an arm of the Tsar's government— a sentiment confirmed by history—and was failing to serve the people. From the renowned author of *War and Peace,* the master of Yasnaya Polyana, this conversion away from the formal Church was a formidable event. To be sure, small groups of sectarians, as well as religious wanderers—dark people, as they were called—dotted the map of Russia, but this was different. This was a heretic, was it not, who now sat in his study at Yasnaya Polyana?

Turgenev came to call on Tolstoy during this time and he records his thoughts in a letter:

"It is an unpardonable sin that Leo Tolstoy has stopped writing—he is a man who could be extraordinarily useful, but what can one do with him? He does not utter a word, and worse than that, he has plunged into mysticism.

Such an artist, such a first-class talent, we have never had, do not now have, among us. I, for instance, am considered an artist, but what am I worth compared to him! In contemporary European literature he has no equal. Whatever he takes up, it all becomes alive under his pen. And how wide the sphere of his creative power—it is simply amazing! . . . But what is one to do with him? He has plunged headlong into another sphere; has surrounded himself with Bibles and Gospels in nearly all languages, and has written a whole heap of papers. He has a trunk full of those mystical ethics and of various pseudo-interpretations. He read me some of it, which I simply do not understand . . . I told him '*That* was not the real thing,' but he replied: 'It is just the real thing.' . . . Very likely he will give nothing more to literature, or if he reappears, it will be with that trunk . . ."[1]

Turgenev was partially right—Tolstoy's religious writing would domi-nate, at least for the next five years. More important, Turgenev identified a conflict which was to last for the rest of Tolstoy's life: the rival claims of the writer and the moralist on his soul. But until 1884, when he began work on his most famous short story, *The Death of Ivan Ilyich,* Leo Tolstoy's creative energies were channeled only toward religious and moral writings. The stuff of the trunk. *The Four Gospels Harmonized* and *What I Believe* were articles issued as pamphlets. He wrote uncompromising works of moral and social reform as well, such as *What Then Must We Do?* (1883), writings posing profound questions that could no longer be avoided by the ruling class or the peasantry. In what Vladimir Nabokov describes as Tolstoy's conflict in which "the artist struggled with the preacher," the preacher now had the upper hand.

Of course the censor was waiting. Indeed the censor was kept busy, for publications questioning the basis of faith in the church was grist for his mill. Since the accession of Alexander III, censorship laws had been tightened and repression of minorities and persecution of independent voices stepped up. *A Confession* had to be put aside for the moment, and only certain sections of the other works passed the censor, but Tolstoy didn't really care. These writings were to solve problems for himself, to disentangle, to find the truth. The search for truth, in Tolstoy's case, had a particularly remorseless quality—no explanation was sufficient, each question led to the next question, a deeper concern, a further debunking of what he called the "general tendency." He was, more than ever, in a period of uncompromising thinking and writing—no hedges, no special consideration, no halfway measures. He was seeking answers to questions of basic human existence. The "vernal shoots" to which he referred in his youth had surfaced; the independence, the egotism, and the need for sweeping inquiry found in the young master of Yasnaya Polyana had come full term.

But had he "plunged headlong into another sphere"? Was Turgenev right about that? Well of course he was right—that is, until the great pagan nature of Tolstoy resurfaced, until he could no longer sit in his study, until a few months after Turgenev's visit when Tolstoy wrote to Fet: "It is now summer and a charming summer, and as usual I go crazy with life and forget my work. This year I struggled long, but the beauty of the world conquered me. I enjoy life and do hardly anything else. Our house is full of visitors. The children have got up theatricals, and it is noisy and merry. I have with difficulty found a corner, and snatched a moment to write to you."[2] What is one to think of this man, who at one point sits silent and ponderous among his Gospels and two months later announces that he is crazy with life and can scarcely concentrate? Does the preacher now give way to the sensualist? Absolutely. In a titanic nature such as Tolstoy's no single emotion could hold him captive. In a divided soul such as his, a permanent battle between the extrovert and the introvert was being waged. Is it possible that the only way Tolstoy could govern his extroverted side was to impose the restrictions of moral perfection?

Records and observations from Yasnaya Polyana of this period show that Tolstoy gave a great deal of his time to the petitions and concerns of the nearby peasants—not just of those on his own estate but of wanderers in from off the road. His diary from the spring of 1881 records: "Today a beggar woman from Kaznacheyvka, drunk. A widow from Grumant. Her boy would do the ploughing. She asked for a horse. I didn't give her one."

This man had better luck: "A crippled old man from Golovenki, a caftan rolled up across his shoulder. Seven roubles for the horse. He wept. Don't wrong people, remember God. I saw him through. Lord have mercy." On June 28: "Back at home, a sick, cross-eyed peasant from Gorodini was waiting for me. A neighbor had brought him in. He was standing waiting in our drive." In another vein, he continues, aware of the irony: "We had an enormous dinner, with champagne. The Tanyas were dressed up. All the children had belts costing five roubles. After dinner, our cart was on its way to a picnic,* surrounded by peasants' carts bringing people back exhausted from work."[3]

---

* Dinner was often at five or six in the afternoon, in summers held as a picnic in the forest. Evening tea followed later, around nine.

A picnic—Tolstoy with family and friends in the park in front of the main house.

To add to the flow of people in off the road, religious wanderers, the "dark people," began appearing. Anyone who wanted to see him could see him. At Yasnaya Polyana, despite the feverish spiritual search going on in his study, Tolstoy received all visitors, all supplicants, and gave any advice that was asked of him.

A saying goes, "The door to a Russian house is always open." The parade to his door, begun back in his childhood as holy fools and wanderers dropped in, now began to swell.

Soon Yasnaya Polyana would become a place of pilgrimage. Eventually the pilgrimage would contribute to the fracturing of the household. But for the moment, the door to Yasnaya was, simply, open. The master received all visitors patiently, perhaps even eagerly.

An entry in Sonya's diary from the mid-1870s reads: "God knows how this year I have had to wrestle with a shameful sense of boredom; how I have tried to remind myself of all that is good in my life, fortifying myself with the thought that country life is much the best thing for both the moral and physical well being of the children."[4]

Tolstoy and group playing tennis, or thinking about playing tennis.

An earlier, more troublesome entry: "I would like to have a good time in frivolous company and new clothes. I want, before it is too late, to be admired . . ."[5] A sense of her state of mind during the early years surrounding Tolstoy's religious obsession can be found in her entry of November 19, 1878: "We had a great to-do with Ilya on Friday. He refused to work and was disobedient and rude to Monsieur Nief, and kept throwing a wet sponge at him . . . In the evening we had quadrilles; the children danced so wholeheartedly; first the older ones, and then the little ones. My sad autumn mood has come over me once again. I sew or read in silence, and feel dull and indifferent to everything, and all the future is dark. The drawing room window is still open; it is foggy but quite warm outside."

In December of 1879 she writes: "Another year has gone past. I am anxiously awaiting for my confinement, which is overdue. The thought of another child depresses me; my whole horizon seems to have narrowed down . . . It has been terribly cold—more than twenty degrees below zero. Masha had a bad throat and a temperature for a week . . ."

And for March 1, 1880: "Andrusha has a cough and still is having attacks of diarrhea at least three times a day. He is pale and weak, and sleeps badly. Misha is constipated; I gave him an enema today." Her mood often darkened to the point of causing "scenes" with Lyovochka, who was puzzled as to why she was so unsympathetic with his religious inquiries. She wrote: "I am feeling very gloomy. Lately I have been having some jealous thoughts and suspicions about Lyovochka. I sometimes feel it is a kind of madness, and keep asking God for help."[6]

By 1881, Sergei, the eldest son, was at the right age for a university education, and Tatyana, age seventeen, was pronounced ready to go into society. Sonya, after eighteen years as keeper of the nursery and general manager of Yasnaya Polyana, finally had the opportunity to bring off a move to Moscow. Tolstoy, to whom city life had always represented vice and impurity, was horrified, even though their stay would only be for the winter months. But he did recognize the necessity for it. In September of 1881, the whole family moved—that is, seven children, servants, tutors, books, and linens—to the first of two houses they were to occupy in Moscow.

The move put a severe strain on an already strained marriage. Tolstoy

Sonya, photographed in Moscow in 1889.

recorded in October, "A month has passed. The most tormenting in my life."

Sonya, in a letter to her sister, gives a fuller accounting: "Tomorrow we shall have been here a month and I have not written a word to anyone. For the first fortnight I cried every day, because Lyovochka not only became depressed, but even fell into a kind of desperate apathy. He did not sleep and did not eat, and sometimes literally wept; I really thought I should go mad. You would be surprised to see how thin I have grown. Afterwards he went to the Province of Tver and visited his old acquaintances . . . and then went to a village to see some sectarian Christian, and when he returned home he was less in the dumps."[7]

She also records that he managed to find some peasants at work by the river, and he joined them chopping wood, which apparently raised his spirits. The sight of Leo Tolstoy, leaving his forty-foot zala, to join the common man at work, was one that interested his disciples and amused his friends—that is, those who could recognize him, for he had by this time completely adapted muzhik dress: sheepskin boots and jacket, simple tunic. He had, in some sense, "taken the cloth."

Tolstoy, in open sledge.

Not only did Tolstoy chop wood with the peasants, which one could easily imagine, but his activities took a different turn: He went into the slums and looked closely into the life of the city's poor. The population of Moscow had swelled since the emancipation of the serfs in 1861, and the oncoming industrialization brought young peasants to the city in search of work. Tolstoy witnessed impoverishment and suffering which even he had never imagined. Almost immediately he requested a position as a volunteer census taker in the most wretched sections of the city. As appalled as he was by the destitution of the poor in the doss houses of Hitrof Market, he was equally upset by the indifference of the rich. And of course one can guess at the effect this huge disparity between rich and poor had on his own inner workings. After a day in the slums, as he sat at table in his splendid house on Dolgo-Khamovnichesky Street, surrounded by comfort, enjoying a five-course dinner as lackeys whisked the food off and on the table and his wife and daughters talked of afternoon visitors and evening balls, of course he was agonized with the injustice of it, beset with guilt. And furious with Sonya for enjoying herself—to the extent that she was able.

What could he do? What of Christian charity?

He immediately tried to raise monies among the rich for general relief. This more or less failed. He attempted to galvanize his fellow census takers, mostly students, toward a more vigorous, charitable attitude. This effort was also frustrated.

He called upon the Gospel according to St. Luke: "And the multitudes asked him, saying, *What then must we do?* He that hath two coats, let him impart to him that hath none; and he that hath food, let him do likewise . . ." Although Tolstoy, at this time, couldn't seem to organize himself and others around the act of doing likewise, he could write a long article about it. And he did.

What Then Must We Do? is a work of some forty short chapters, a chronicle of city culture, life in dark places, rousing thoughts of reform, touching interviews, raw incidents. New territory for Tolstoy. He began *What Then Must We Do?* in 1882 and finished it two years later. Like other pieces of his written that year (*On the Moscow Census* and *What I Believe*), this was a long piece, full of urgency, the moral questions framed with great simplicity. The net effect of this harrowing treatise was to broaden his indignation on the subject of social organization and injustice and to arouse the conscience of many, the beginning, in his case, of his ability to stamp his thoughts into the daily lives of his countrymen.

After a few months (and off and on at various intervals throughout the winter), he left Moscow and returned alone for a time to Yasnaya Polyana and the simple life. Leaving Sonya in charge (by now an established habit), he wrote to her: "I think that I could nowhere be better off or more tranquil. You, who are always at home and occupied with family cares, cannot feel the difference the town and country make to me."[8] (Indeed she surely could.)

In the year 1882, Tolstoy made two decisions connected with his new simplified life; he gave his wife legal power of attorney to conduct all matters of decisions concerning his property, and he dropped the use of his title.

The first act was a simple dodge to remove him from the sin of property. How could he own land and live off the work of others? Authority passed to the hands of his wife was a most imperfect solution, however, for he still held title to the land. The internal conflict surrounding his ownership of Yasnaya Polyana was a problem which grew to gigantic proportions, but the use of Sonya as power of attorney let him off the hook for a while. But just for a while.

The title proved a lesser problem. There was a great deal of bowing and scraping in prerevolutionary Russia. Hats were doffed to the nobility, and the formal manner of address, *vashe syatyelslvo,* which translates to mean "Your Luminousness," was scrupulously observed. In the twentieth century we have absorbed, in those few countries where it is still necessary, the use of the title "Your Majesty," but to our ears "Your Luminousness" does seem somewhat elevated. Not so in nineteenth-century Russia.[9] Lofty address and windy titles were numerous—and not easily abandoned. But from that moment on, Tolstoy would cheerfully remind his visitors that they were to call him Lev Nikolayevich. Nothing more.

It was at about this time that Tolstoy took up boot making. As part of the simple life, he felt that manual labor and the stitching of one's own shoes was essential. The working of the scythe had always come easily to him; he could mow in the fields for hours on end and only feel exhilarated. But cutting, nailing, stitching his own boots was a different matter. Weary of his own moral writings ("How terrible the polemic bitterness is," he recorded in his diary), he now plunged into the work of the cobbler. Both at Yasnaya Polyana and in the Moscow house, boot making instruction took place, yet it is not clear whether this activity ever gave him real satisfaction. In the many books about Tolstoy, endless reference is made to his boot making and to the picture of him at his work table, struggling with his tools. This was the public image of him—the aristocrat doing the work of the humble man. In the great artist Ilya Repin's most famous picture of him, he is at the plough. In fact, although in our cynical twentieth century we might find the picture of the wellborn gentleman sewing up his own boots a little pious, this and other images of Tolstoy were extremely popular at that time. Everyone loved the count who ploughed his own fields, who dressed like a muzhik. A legend was in the making. As to the results of his cobbling, who knows, since only the master himself wore his handiwork, but boot making seemed to draw him closer to the "bright and morally refined" work of the simple man.

Although winters were spent *en famille* in Moscow, Tolstoy often returned to Yasnaya Polyana, the only place where life was really bearable for him. The whole family regrouped back at Yasnaya for all holidays and the long summer vacation. Spliced in between diary references to bathing in the river and picnics and new governesses, we begin to feel the real undertow of discord between Tolstoy and his wife and, as well, the beginning of "scenes," accompanied by threats and hysterics. The restraint and coolness so often associated with the English aristocracy had no play in Russian estate life. Daily emotions were acted upon. In 1882, at Yasnaya Polyana, Sonya made this entry:

"For the first time in my life, Lyova has run away from me and has spent the night in his study. We quarreled over mere trifles; I blame him for not taking a sufficient interest in the children, for not helping me . . . He cried aloud today that his most passionate desire was to get away from his family. To my last breath I shall remember this candid exclamation which seemed to tear out my heart. I am begging God to let me die, for I cannot live without his love; I realized that the moment his love vanished. I can't tell him how much I love him—it is the same love which I have given him all these twenty years. It humiliates *me* and annoys *him*. He is full of Christianity and the idea of self-perfection . . . God help me! I want to kill myself—my thoughts are all confused. The clock is striking four. If he doesn't come back I shall know he loves another woman." Later, although Tolstoy did come back, and of course there was no other woman, Sonya wandered out to the pond anyway, where she "stayed for a long time in the ice water, hoping to catch a chill and die."[10]

Had Sonya been blessed with a sense of humor it is possible that she could have ridden out some of these quarrels over *trifles* which ended in such drama. Though she was prone to flights of romantic self-pity, it is hard not to feel moved by the wife who was overburdened and whose thoughts were "all confused." Love is not rational. Russian domestic life ran on deeply furrowed emotions. It could not have been easy to be married to a man of Tolstoy's volatility, egotism, and soaring Christianity. It is important to note that they did have reconciliations. They could still make peace. Sonya was pregnant with Alexandra in 1884, the year of their worst discord.

On April 4 of that year Tolstoy's diary reads: "It's very depressing in the family. Depressing, because I can't sympathize with them. All their joys, the examination, social success, music, furniture, shopping—I consider them all a misfortune and an evil for them, and I can't tell them so. I can and do speak, but my words don't get through to anyone . . . They must see that for three years now I've not merely suffered, but been cut off from life. I've been assigned the role of the querulous old man in their eyes and I can't escape from it."[11]

May 3: "Poor Sonya, how she hates me. Lord, help me. If this is my cross, let it weigh me down and crush me. But this harassment of my soul is terrible . . ."[12]

June 10: "It is awful that the luxury, the corruption of life in which I live, I myself have created, and I am myself corrupted and I cannot reform it . . ."[13]

June 18: "In the evening I did some mowing near the house. A peasant came about the estate. Went for a bath. Came back cheerful and in good spirits, and suddenly there began some absurd reproaches on my wife's part about the horses which I don't need and which I only want to get rid of. I said nothing but was terribly depressed. I left, and wanted to leave for good, but her pregnancy made me turn back half-way to Tula." In fact, Tolstoy had thrown some things in a knapsack and started on foot to Tula, threatening to "move to America."[14]

The need for flight. "*I wanted to leave for good.*" The temptation of flight, his flight from Sonya, from Yasnaya Polyana, here establishes itself. This pattern would haunt her and follow them both through to the end of his life.

As to his ability to *get through to* the children on the joys of Spartan living, no one, then or now, could possibly expect much success in this task. A family raised on the abundance of gentry living, surrounded with the trappings of wealth and privilege, suddenly finds its patriarch filled with stern remorse and frugal Christianity—that they were puzzled and that he felt "cut off" cannot be surprising.

Their daughter Tanya gives us a picture of life in the zala after dinner: "In the evening Papa was arguing with Mamma and Auntie Tanya, and said lovely things about his view on good living, saying that riches prevent goodness. Then Mamma cut it all short and said we must go to bed . . . I was just going when he stopped us and we stood talking another whole hour. He holds that . . . we squander our finest feelings on dress. I said I quite agreed, and rationally I understood it all and would like to live properly, but my emotional side remains completely unmoved by anything that is good, while at the promise of a new frock or a new hat my heart leaps . . . There was a lot more I wanted to ask, but I could not speak, I was crying so, yet there was nothing to cry about in it, was there?"[15]

Another ominous entry from Tolstoy's diary of 1884: ". . . she [Sonya] came to my room and started an hysterical scene—the sense of it being that nothing can be changed, and she is unhappy . . . I was sorry for her, but at the same time I was aware that it was hopeless. She will remain a mill-stone around my neck and the children's until I die."[16]

This final entry on September 15: "Went to look for mushrooms. Miserable."[17]

In the middle of this emotional morass an eager, twenty-nine-year-old disciple, an army officer named Vladimir Grigoryevich Chertkov, presented himself. Unlike most of the ragged worshipers who came to call, he was handsome, rich, and wellborn. In the tradition of the aristocracy, his early youth had been pampered and frivolous, and in the middle of his twenties he had changed course, moved to the country, and sought a new Christianity for himself; he had read and was fascinated by Tolstoy. Chertkov was headed to Yasnaya Polyana to make a pilgrimage when a mutual friend told him that Tolstoy was in Moscow. He hastened to Dolgo-Khamovnichesky Street. Chertkov believed he was seeking a spiritual father. Tolstoy, unknowingly, needed a spiritual son. Their meeting was short but fortuitous and bore with it lasting implications for them all.

At first, Sonya quite liked Chertkov. He was from an aristocratic family, he treated her with deference, and his mother was an intimate of the empress. He certainly represented an improvement on the now-increasing numbers of disciples who cluttered the entryway in Moscow or flocked up the tree-lined *prospekt* of Yasnaya Polyana to talk with the master.

An intensity of feeling between Tolstoy and Chertkov developed almost

Vladimir Chertkov.

instantly. Tolstoy referred to his young new disciple as his co-thinker, which was quite something to say about someone whom he had just met; it suggests, perhaps, from this giant of an individual, that he truly *wanted* a co-thinker. Visits were frequent, but letters were more so. It seems that both men found particular spiritual release in their correspondence. Chertkov's devotion to the master's teachings had a zeal and perhaps a narrow-mindedness which made Tolstoy skeptical as early as March of 1884. ". . . I am afraid you are carried away by proselytism—by conversion as an end in itself. Conversion is only effective and is only accomplished when it is the consequence (almost unconscious) of one's own consolidation and therefore improvement," he warned.[18] The handsome disciple's earnestness did find a practical outlet, however, and with Tolstoy's blessing and encouragement Chertkov started a publishing house, Posrednik, or the Intermediary, devoted to making Tolstoy's writings available to the masses at modest prices. Later, Tolstoy would write and contribute his lovely, simple parables, *Twenty-three Tales,* to the Intermediary for distribution.

The correspondence between the two, in the beginning weighty with spiritual and philosophic exchange, took on a more personal nature. Tolstoy wrote to him in December 1885: ". . . I am sorely heavy at heart, and there is nobody I wish to share this heaviness with as much as you dear friend, because it seems to me that nobody loves the good that there is in me as much as you . . . I haven't been writing these last few days, and I'm still not writing and that is why I look around me and judge myself and am horrified." He spoke of his own unhappiness within his family: "If I begin to talk to my wife or my eldest son, the result is malice, plain malice against which I am weak and which infects me as well. But what is better for me to do? To put up with it and to lie, as I lie now with my whole life—sitting at the table, lying in bed, allowing the sale of my works, signing papers about voting rights, allowing peasants to be punished and persecuted for stealing my property, on my authority? Or to make a complete break—and give way to anger?"[19]

If this letter seems to find Tolstoy quite sorry for himself, it found in Chertkov a most willing ally. Eagerly, he took up the post as Tolstoy's principal confidant in domestic matters. Instinctively, he sympathized with the master's belief that he was truly suffering at the hands of the philistines—that is, Sonya and the children.

There can be no doubt that Tolstoy's relationship with Chertkov was of great importance to him, consistent through periods of exile, through illness, and long periods of spiritual joining. Chertkov edited his works, encouraged the purist's side of his Christianity, and laid balm on his suffering. Sonya contained her suspicions about Chertkov at first to a simple diary entry, on March 6, 1887: "We have a letter from Chertkov. I do not like him; he is clever and sly and one-sided, and not a good man."[20] The struggle between them for Tolstoy's soul began quietly.

"I went out today at eleven, and was intoxicated by the beauty of the morning. It was warm and dry. Here and there in the frost-graze of the footpaths, little spikes and tufts of grass show up from under the dead leaves and straw; the buds are swelling on the lilacs, the birds no longer sing at random, but have already begun to converse about something, and round the sheltered corners of the house and by manure heaps, bees are humming. I saddled my horse and rode out. In the afternoon I read, then went to the apiary and the bathing house. Everywhere grass, birds, honey-bees; no policemen, no pavement, no cabmen, no stinks, and it is very pleasant—so pleasant that I grow sorry for you and think that you and the children must certainly come here earlier . . ."[21]

This was written to Sonya from Yasnaya Polyana. By 1885 Tolstoy had

Tolstoy walks on bridge of nearby property.

found a way to combine his love for his estate, perhaps his only perfect love, with his desire to involve his family in the new simple life. Manual labor. Manual labor *for everybody.*

That same year, he wrote several short stories and parables and continued his moral preachings in letter and pamphlet form: *Industry and Idleness,* written as a preface to a book by a peasant-sectarian named Bondaref; and in letter form, in an essay called *Manual Labor,* he gives summary to his thinking: "... Of all the definite duties of man, the chief, primary and most immutable for every man, is to earn his bread with his own hands, understanding by 'bread-labour'—all heavy rough work necessary to save man from death ..."[22] At Yasnaya Polyana, the number of drop-in disciples began to swell as Tolstoyan principles and publications received wider circulation. To Sonya's annoyance, new Tolstoyans gathered in the fields at night and, by the new day's light, proceeded like a small army to the main house to catch a glimpse of the master and begin the work of ploughing. Joining this steady stream were an occasional few who *did not* sleep in the fields: neighbors, some friends of Chertkov's, and, most important—family. The Tolstoy family was now pitching in. The Austrian governess, Anna Seuron, made notes and gives us this account:

> Haymaking! What a picture! Counts, Princes, teachers, and all sorts of blue-blooded people tried to work in competition with the peasants. Scythes hacked awkwardly, mowing the sappy grass. Everyone strove to outdo the others. As far as the eye could reach, workers were seen everywhere. All the peasants were there, and so was the Countess, in a Russian dress; children and governesses— we all helped to turn the hay. The hunting dogs lay around, and a specially hot sun shone on the smiling meadow. In the distance, on one hill was seen the village, and on another, the Count's house.
>
> And there he stands, that peasant Count, in a Russian shirt and trousers, his legs wide apart, mowing; and looking at him, I can see that he is quite engrossed in it. He is listening to the sound of the scythes, and enjoying himself.

Yes, by all that is just, he was enjoying himself, for it really was only under these idyllic circumstances, family and peasant together, mowing, joined with nature, working the fields, that he could allow himself to feel content.

Consistent with his new faith and the simple life, he began, systematically, to give up things that he cared for. Anna Seuron, a somewhat acid observer, makes note of his various renunciations ("the count seemed possessed by a fever of renunciation"): Red meat. Salt. Hunting and shooting, his primary passions.

And tobacco. Anyone who has ever had to give up smoking can but sympathize: "He suffered unendurable torment, positively not knowing what to do with himself. He would pick up a cigarette-end here and there, like a schoolboy, have but a single whiff; or dilating his nostrils, he would eagerly inhale the smoke when others smoked in his presence. After a while, despite his convictions, he would again yield to his inclinations . . ."[23]

While suffering his own torment, the puritan in him was still able to guide the fate of others. In his 1911 biography of Tolstoy, Nathan Haskell Dole describes what well may have been the first Slavic Alcoholics Anonymous meeting on record:

In 1887, Tolstoi's interest was awakened in the cause of temperance among the people. He ordered the starosta [the village leader] of the village to summon all the inhabitants to the village at ten in the morning. A table and bench were placed before the communal house. When all were present he gave them a lecture in plain simple language on the dangers of drunkenness, on the evils that followed the use of tobacco and vodka. He spoke slowly and persuasively, urging arguments that would appeal to peasant folk and introducing striking anecdotes and similes.

The women urged their husbands to follow Tolstoi's advice; so, seeing that he had them on his side, he asked those that would agree henceforth to drink no more to sign the pledge.

"Do you consent?" he cried.

Just at that moment a harsh voice sounded: 'Let me pass.'

"Room for Yegor Ivanuitch," cried the peasants, and an old muzhik stepped forward.

"I want to speak a word about temperance," he said. "I want to call your attention to the fact that at weddings, births and baptisms, it is impossible to get along without vodka. One can do without smoking, but vodka—that is different. It is necessary, it is indispensable . . . Our fathers always drank it; we must do the same."

"You can substitute sugared rose water," replied Tolstoi. "In the south, rose water is always served with sherbets thick as honey."

"Does that make men drunk?" asked many at once.

"No! Then do you agree?" asked the count again.

"Yes, yes!"

The muzhiks crowded up to the table; the women were radiant; even the children seemed to realize that something great was happening; the idea of sugared rose water enchanted them.[24]

History would argue that rose water is a substitute for absolutely nothing, particularly in Russia, but Tolstoy's quest for a state of grace drove him on. Apparently, the mere sight of him inspired others; Anna Seuron suggests that anyone witnessing the count's sudden thinness "could easily have convinced himself that this too was one of the paths to salvation."

The regime of Alexander III was repressive,* and the work of salvation may have seemed quite desirable to many burdened Russian citizens. Industrial Russia had begun a slow, painful rise; famine stalked the countryside. Slavic predisposition toward physical brutality continued and the practice of flogging and running the gauntlet were constant, resulting in an ongoing fear and bitterness by all citizens toward authority.

Exempt from blame was of course the one figure who was surely responsible—the Tsar. Alexander III was stern, suspicious, narrow, and "when he spoke, he gave the impression of being on the point of striking you." The personality of the Tsar *was* policy. In this total autocracy, there were no forces to balance, let alone curtail his authority. But the people of Russia saw the reigning monarch as truly above all others, ruling by divine authority, and while they might occasionally affix blame for their woeful circumstances on one or two of his ministers, he himself was Batiushka Tsar—the Little Father Tsar. Even the intelligentsia hedged, aware of the speed with which a hangman's noose could be drawn, the torment of a prison sentence or exile. Assassins always lay in wait; but in the case of Alexander III, who could twist a silver fork into a knot with one hand, they were cautious. In 1887, five were hanged for an attempt on the Tsar's life. Among them: Lenin's brother, Alexander Ulyanov.

The figure of Konstantin Petrovich Pobedonostsev contributed to the cruel and stagnant atmosphere of the moment. As procurator of the Holy Synod, he had a general contempt for the peasant and an utter rigidity on matters of orthodoxy within the Russian church. Censorship was strict. Hope for any form of parliamentarianism seemed remote. The liberals lay low.

Into this atmosphere of repression and harshness strode the person of Lev Nikolayevich Tolstoy, bearing with him the gospels of a new Christianity based on brotherly love, asking his fellow man to search for truth and to "hold together unconsciously." It is not hard to understand why he and his preaching became so popular. And with the adroit hand of Chertkov now publishing his moral writings and tales for the masses, Tolstoy, by the end of the 1880s, had developed a huge, respectful following. He seemed to be able to draw the moral center to him, to wherever he was. It is fair to say that for many people, particularly the peasantry, Tolstoy represented the only voice of hope and

---

* Alexander abandoned such reforms as limited trial by jury and university rights, reinstating use of the rod, public executions, and execution of political prisoners.

Tolstoy walks among his beloved birch trees.

protection—and he seemed to offer protection—in the land at that moment. He seemed godlike, larger than life to many. The writer Maxim Gorky visited him often in the later years. Gorky describes Tolstoy's "disproportionately overgrown individuality . . . there is in him something of the *bogatyr* [a brave but wild and self-willed child] which the earth can't hold."

Yet, Gorky continues, "He is like a god, not a Sabaoth or Olympian, but the kind of Russian god who sits on a maple throne under a golden lime tree, not very majestic, but perhaps more cunning than all the other gods."[25]

By the end of the 1880s the number of visitors (uninvited) to Yasnaya had dramatically increased. The poor, the supplicants, and the wanderers were in the habit of gathering near the house at Yasnaya, under a huge maple tree where hung the dinner bell; Tree of the Poor, it was called. There they waited for advice, or a rouble or two from the master. Not only simple Russians but "those oppressed by riches and ennui, came in carriages, on horseback or on foot," to seek counsel. Anna Seuron tells us that "all classes of society wandered in at those entrance gates near the high road, which, in spite of neglect— spoke of grander times."[26]

Grander times, and uncomplicated times, when the division of classes was inviolate, when the church was unquestioned, when the landed gentry held easily onto the reins—when no one doubted that the estate would simply pass to each new generation of Tolstoys.

What had been an island of some calm in Tolstoy's life was now drawn into question. Yasnaya Polyana, birthplace of his mother, scene of his childhood, was also a place where peasants worked the land, over which he, the landowning aristocrat, held title and power. From their sweat came his income. The issue of what to do with the ownership of Yasnaya Polyana had come to plague its patriarch.

In 1884, his diary records that he talked with Sonya ("a cruel conversation") in an attempt to persuade her that they should give up the revenues from the vast property in Samara—that he not profit from distant labors of the peasants—and try to live more frugally on the sparse revenues from Yasnaya Polyana. Tolstoy's ultimate objective was to give the majority of his land to the peasants. Sonya believed that the ownership of land came from a holy mandate. She was also a woman of sure practicality; with this huge family they needed every rouble they could get. That forced the focus back on Yasnaya. "We have property on a false basis of private ownership," Tolstoy told his disbelieving wife, and he proposed a plan of reducing his ownership by degrees. He had been strongly influenced about this time by the writings of an American, the social reformer Henry George, who advocated the end of private ownership and the idea of a one-time tax on leased land, called the single tax theory. "Property is the root of all evil," Tolstoy wrote in *What Then Must We Do?* "States, governments, intrigue and go to war for property . . . Bankers, traders, manufacturers and landowners work, scheme and torment themselves and others for property; officials and peasants struggle, cheat, oppress and suffer for the sake of property."[27] His thought was to keep the house and nearby gardens, for which he designed a pattern of existence based on physical labor, absolutely no luxury, and women and men dressed simply, living in separate quarters. Even those sympathetic to Tolstoy could find little to love in this last plan.

The sin of property was not new; it was a huge issue and impossible to resolve. It took a revolution to accomplish its end in Russia, and it is doubtful that this major tenet of modern-day communism—that of no private ownership—will survive the 1990s. In the Tolstoy household, giving away his land meant changing an entire way of life for his family; it could not be compared to the abandoning of tobacco or salt. Yasnaya Polyana was the very center of their universe, it held the structure of life in place. Could it be given away, even by degrees? Without the fruits of the land, how could the Tolstoys live?

His neighbors and his critics ridiculed the patriarch of Yasnaya Polyana for continuing to absorb the comforts of a landowner while preaching what were essentially the virtues of communal life—brotherhood, shared responsibility, simplicity, renunciation of the use of money.

Throughout the many assaults on him from the doubters and those who cried hypocrite, Tolstoy remained adamant. He was not one to hedge, and practical questions did not interest him. He believed that at the heart of the matter lay a concern which was not unreasonable: Land is a gift of nature—a

A quick game of gorodki *(a kind of outdoor bowling), while the son of a servant looks on.*

free gift of nature—in which all men should have an equal right to ownership. To release his lands to those who had tilled that same soil for generations did seem to him to be logical and just. What did the Gospels say? "Sell all that you have and distribute it to the poor" (Luke 18:18–25).

Tolstoy's ability to find the heart of the matter did not make life any easier for him, or for those around him. As Chertkov urged him forward, prodding him to live the life he preached, Sonya made the case that their expenses were, if anything, on the rise. She had been trained, after all, by tradition and *by her husband* to serve as a landowner's wife, with freewheeling hospitality, picnics, cooks, tutors, and the prospect of light lifting as far as future work for her children. She had managed skillfully. She had borne him twelve children. By the end of the 1880s, Sonya became openly hostile to the simple life and particularly vehement when it came to talk of distributing land to the peasants.

The household at Yasnaya Polyana now seemed to divide itself into two warring camps: For Sonya and her sons, the old order was good enough. In the opposite corner, Leo Tolstoy was joined by his daughter Masha, with Alexandra soon to become his most ardent follower. The great grace of Tatyana Lyovovna, the oldest daughter, was tested but not found wanting, as she steered a path through the war zone and managed to keep peace with both of her parents.

"My friend, go back to literature!"

Turgenev lay dying. His last note to Tolstoy in the summer of 1883 bore with it an urgent and moving message: "Dear Lev Nikolayevich, I have not written you for a long time, for, to be frank, I have been and am still, on my death bed. I can never get well, it is useless to think about it. I am writing to tell you how happy I was to have been your contemporary, and to make you one last request. My friend, go back to literature. It is your gift, which comes whence comes all else. Ah, how happy I should be if I could believe that my words would influence you!"[28]

It isn't clear whether his words did have influence. Although Tolstoy did, in later years, heap unconvincing scorn on his own fiction, at this time in the mid-eighties he did not consider that he had altogether abandoned his fiction for moral writings; as well, in all of his earlier fiction, moral purpose could be found throughout. And in this most complicated relationship with Turgenev, where they were either quarreling or writing each other letters full of love, one can only conclude that theirs was a profound friendship, full of misunderstanding, that did not require consistency. Oddly, Tolstoy did not answer Turgenev's note, or he didn't answer it on time, for Turgenev died a few weeks later.

Nonetheless, in the year 1886, Tolstoy published a short story, *The Death of Ivan Ilyich,* which was so powerful, so profound in its implications, that whether he was in any way responsible or not, Turgenev would have been pleased. And critics who suggested that Tolstoy was washed up as a great fiction writer have the ghost of Ivan Ilyich to haunt them.

A middle-aged bureaucrat, Ivan Ilyich falls off a ladder in his newly decorated apartment, and therein begins a slow, painful, and certain march toward his death months later. The story, which is long (some seventy pages), is not only an agonizing account of his sickness and his internal torment, but it is also about the empty life that he has led. A life of petty concerns, officialdom, the ultimate bourgeois, "comme il faut" existence. Ivan Ilyich feels the impatience of his wife and family with his suffering and his decaying body. He is terrified. Only death and blackness await him, and as he lies on his couch in pain, the truth of his meaningless, empty life sweeps over him. Nothing can bring him comfort. Only the manservant, Gerassim, a strapping youth without a trace of hypocrisy, can relieve his pain, however fleetingly. Moments before death, Ivan is overcome by a vision: "Where is death? What Death? He was not afraid any more because there was no death any more. Instead of death, there was only light." And thus he passes through life, leaving not a trace of himself imprinted on one single soul.

The Death of Ivan Ilyich was ecstatically received. Reading this story, one feels its physical and emotional force to such a degree that it is sometimes hard to get one's breath. There is a tendency on the part of teachers and critics to suggest that everything Tolstoy wrote is a masterpiece; but *The Death of Ivan Ilyich* really is one. It is concise, large of vision, and ironic, and its implications are universal. Ivan Ilyich is an Everyman, harboring the Master's concerns.

The composer Tchaikovsky, who had come to know Tolstoy at around the time of *Anna Karenina,* wrote in his diary: "Read the *Death of Ivan Ilyich.* More than ever I am convinced that the greatest of all artist-writers is L. N. Tolstoy." He referred to "the eternally great, almost divine, significance of Tolstoy."[29] And Sonya was swept with relief. With *The Death of Ivan Ilyich,* his creative hand was back. Lyovochka was doing that which he was meant to do.

Tolstoy gave the story to her as a gift. She was pleased. Now it could be included in her new, massive effort—publishing the complete works of Leo Tolstoy. Chertkov and his friends at the Intermediary couldn't put their hands on this one.

Three years later, Tolstoy wrote *The Kreutzer Sonata*. That proved to be a different kind of gift.

Strangers on a train are drawn to listen to a confession by Pózdnyshev, who, in a moment of violent jealousy, has killed his wife. As he recounts his story, he vents his rage against sexual love and women's power over men. *The Kreutzer Sonata* is a mean tale, despite its affecting moments. It is a story of pathological jealousy and hatred. At its core is the emphatic suggestion that marriage is just another form of prostitution. Pózdnyshev murders his wife after he suspects her of infidelity with a visitor. Yet, she and her caller have only been playing Beethoven's Kreutzer Sonata.

The story was copied out and widely distributed before the censor had a look at it; in St. Petersburg and Moscow, questions it raised were on everyone's lips. Was it true that Tolstoy believed that in order to lead a truly Christian life one must turn to chastity? Was not marriage a Christian concept? Before he wrote *The Kreutzer Sonata* Tolstoy had become enchanted with descriptions of the Shaker colonies in America. Yes, he felt chastity was a fine idea to purify the heart or to combat weakness of the flesh. In the middle of the writing of this treatise on the sins of the flesh and the unworthiness of marriage, Sonya gave birth to a thirteenth child, a boy, Ivan, whom they called Vanichka.

"You say that the women of our society have other interests in life than prostitutes have, but I say no and I will prove it," says Pózdnyshev in the beginning of the tale. The bitterest vendetta against women follows, a diatribe, of course made dramatic and absorbing by the genius of Tolstoy, yet a diatribe it is. All of the accepted rites of love, marriage, children, and domestic life are reviled and mocked. No novel of manners is *The Kreutzer Sonata*.

"We were like two convicts hating each other and chained together, poisoning one another's lives and trying not to see it," says Pózdnyshev of life with his wife. A life of quarrels, temptations, hostility. "I think of running away from her, hiding myself, going to America."[30] In one of many recognizable moments from Tolstoy's own life, the miserable Pózdnyshev adds,

"Just when we find life together unendurable, it becomes necessary to move to town for the children's education."

One can only imagine Sonya's thoughts as she sat copying out these passages. No, in fiction, the characters are invented—Pózdnyshev was not Tolstoy and the wife was not Sonya—but, as in all of his works, there is clear autobiographical detail, and the implications were damning. In her diary Sonya records: "I don't know why and how they have connected *The Kreutzer Sonata* with our married life, and yet it is a fact that everybody—from the Tsar right down to Lyovochka's brother and his best friend Dyakov—have felt sorry for me. But what's the good of looking at other people? In my own heart I have felt that this story was directed against me; it has wounded me and has disgraced me in the eyes of the whole world, and has destroyed the last remnant of love between us."[31]

The censor was quick to jump on *The Kreutzer Sonata,* but private copyists had been quick, too, and the story was out in public. How could Sonya dispel the implication of hatred and turmoil in the Tolstoy household? She would go directly to the Tsar herself; she, the supposed victim, would plead for the release of the story. The Tsar could cancel the censor with a wave of the hand. Her act of intervention on behalf of the book would surely clear her from its implications. Or would it?

Thanks to her visit to the Tsar, *The Kreutzer Sonata* was released for publication. Many detested the story, and the church objected to it violently. But everyone read it. Anton Chekhov, whose first volume of short stories had just been published, said, "It is hardly possible to find anything of equal importance either in conception or beauty of execution."[32] And apparently, so susceptible was a segment of the population that chastity gained some ground among young Russians as a result.

In March Sonya wrote in her diary: "If only the people who read *The Kreutzer Sonata* with such feeling of veneration could look for a moment at the erotic life he lives—and which alone makes him happy and cheerful—they would cast this little God from the pedestal on which they have placed him. And yet I love him best when he is weak and kind and normal in his habits."[33]

One could well speculate that Tolstoy's puritanism, now blended with rank intolerance, was the only force by which he could try to control his own erotic nature. Sexual passion had gone unbridled in his youth, had tormented him, had always made him feel guilty, and now found him locked in marriage with a woman for whom he had rushes of hatred. And he needed her still. "I'm writing this at a time [May 1891] when I'm possessed myself by sexual desire, against which I can't fight."[34]

Tolstoy's torment went on. The pagan and the radical Christian continued their interior struggle. Tolstoy was sixty-three.

6

A TASTE FOR PUBLIC ACTION
[1890–1901]

As the 1880s drew to a close, the landholding gentry unquestionably began to feel the march of time—a march not going in their direction. County councils, called zemstvos, established in the 1860s, had taken on some of the responsibilities held informally in the past by important landowners—that is, distribution of food, supervision of hospitals, allotment of funds for schools—in short, the work of the zemstvos challenged the authority, and therefore the life, of the gentry class. Peasants made up about 40 percent in the distribution of seats on the zemstvos. Of course the landowners held a majority, but the peasants had a voice.

From their meager land allotments, many peasants fled to the cities to try to make some money, soon to join an emerging proletarian class. In the country, estates that were loosely managed (which meant most of them, including Yasnaya Polyana) were having trouble making ends meet. To counter the control of the local councils and to protect the landowners, in 1890 the government of Tsar Alexander III decided to give increased power to court-appointed provincial governors over the local zemstvo councils. The tsar also opened a special bank for the nobility, to help preserve the landed properties, as they slid increasingly into debt. The peasantry, ever crafty and suspicious of their masters, bargained, resisted, and often refused to work for miserable wages. As the United States learned in the South after the Civil War, a way of life can reverse itself without one of its principal components— indentured labor.

Russia began to establish herself as an industrial state, but inevitable chaos and deprivation followed as a result of moving the economy away from an essentially agrarian way of life. Prices rose sharply, and taxes were raised, even though there was often less to collect; the Russian method of tax collection included a sweep through town by cossack soldiers brandishing sabers and whipping rods. By 1890 many parts of Russia suffered an agrarian crisis— in other words, massive famine.

How did the famine affect life at Yasnaya Polyana? Sonya gives us a feel for the moment in her diary entry of 13 June 1891: ". . . It is very cold at night but the days are dry and hot. It is very painful to hear on all sides complaints about the drought and the growing famine. I can't see how the Russian people

Merriment in 1896. Left to right: A. A. Shkarvan, with Alexander Behrs on his shoulders, M. Bonnet-Maurie, N. L. Obolensky, Tatyana, manservant, Chertkov, Tolstoy, A. N. Dunayev. Seated: Governess M. Auber, Masha, Alexandra, Sonya.

will pull through this year, for, in some parts, the corn has failed completely, and the ground has had to be ploughed all over again. Yasnaya Polyana is not so badly off, but in some parts of the country there will be no food for either man or beast. After dinner, I tidied the house, and Formich and Nikita helped me sweep the rubbish out of all the corners; then I called Ivan Alexandrovich and the gardener, and we went out to count the apples and to calculate the probable yield per tree. This went on till night, and tomorrow I shall start again.

"We spent the evening on the verandah, drinking tea and feeling cold . . ." If the worst of it was the tedium of counting apples, we can tell ourselves that Yasnaya Polyana, protected against misfortune, continued at its own enchanted pace.[1]

Tolstoy was slow to come to terms with the famine, this massive, disastrous threat to the life of his countrymen. From his cool first-floor study, he was preoccupied with his writings, and a family crisis was gathering force around the touchy subject of the distribution of his property. Tolstoy's ambition—to give his land to the peasants—had met with predictable howls of resistance from all of his sons, as well as Sonya. Therefore, he decided that, as he felt that it was unconscionable for him to own property in any form, and to give it away to the peasantry did in fact rob his children of a way of life, he would simply parcel it out to his offspring as if he were writing a will, give away the booty while he was still alive, thus preventing any further reference to the matter of property and legacies. Little did he know at that time, in July of 1891, how potent and resilient the subject of his will would be.

Leo Tolstoy's potentially huge holdings, encompassing the properties at Nikolskoye and Grinevka, the vast acreage in Samara, the Moscow house, and of course Yasnaya Polyana, were divided up into ten shares. One for Sonya and one for each of the nine living children. (Masha, her father's favorite, nobly refused her share. Later she married a penniless nobleman and had to ask for it back.) Each of the erstwhile shareholders, except Masha, spent long afternoons backing and forthing and jockeying for, in this case, acreage, and poor old Tolstoy suffered with each new round. He wrote, "I've been staying on [at Yasnaya Polyana] for the division of the property. It's depressing, terribly painful. I pray that God will rescue me . . . Yesterday there was an astonishing conversation among the children, Tanya and Lyova were suggesting to Masha that she was playing a mean trick by refusing her property. Her conduct makes them feel the wrongness of their own, but they must be in the

Tolstoy with his sister, Marya, who had become a nun.

right themselves so they invent reasons why her conduct is bad and a mean trick. It's terrible. I can't write. I wept, and I could weep again. They say, 'We would like to do it ourselves, but it would be wrong.' My wife says, 'Leave it to me!' It's terrible! I've never seen lies and the motives for them so palpably obvious. I'm sad, sad, and sorely depressed."[2]

A month later the division of his assets was finished. Now he lived in closer accord with his principles, eating his kasha (a simple gruel), cleaning his own room, emptying his own chamber pot, and berating himself for his remaining luxuries.

The issue of the property was but a curtain-raiser to the anguish raised on the subject of the copyrights of his works. The royalties already collected by Sonya for his *Complete Works* had been substantial. Was this to be part of the distribution too? After a series of scenes, shouting, suicide threats, and finally, reconciliation, Tolstoy, now only seeking peace, made a compromise and sent a letter to the most prominent Russian newspapers stating that all works that he wrote after the year 1881, the year of his "rebirth," were free of copyright, in the public domain. The mammoth works preceding 1881, *War and Peace* and *Anna Karenina,* were to be held in copyright by Sonya. Thus the

Family group on porch, photographed in 1892. Left to right: *guest, Andrei, Tolstoy, Alexandra, Lev, Masha, Sonya, and Vanichka.*

family coffers could continue to be filled. The matter of copyright went into dormancy but was far from concluded. Leo Tolstoy was, on paper at least, divested of the evils of property.

In the larger world the famine raged on. A longtime friend, Ivan Ivonovich Rayevsky, was among the many visitors in the summer of 1891, and he began to persuade Tolstoy to let go his rather lofty creed that "a good deed does not consist in giving bread to feed the famished, but in loving the famished. Loving is more important than giving food."[3]

The famine was ravaging the countryside and Rayevsky was persistent— go and look for yourself, he advised.

Once the master of Yasnaya Polyana started touring the villages in the southwestern provinces, his distant Christianity was disturbed. "On the 24th we walked to the village of Meshcherki. The run down state of the people is dreadful; ruined houses—there was a fire last year—they don't have anything, but they still drink. They are like children who laugh when they get into trouble. Towards evening Bogoyavlensky and Rayevsky came. I decided to settle in with Rayevsky. It would be good if Sonya didn't object. I even left ninety roubles to buy potatoes and beets."[4]

He went to work. Leo Tolstoy had never been much of what we might today call an administrator, but he joined Rayevsky at his place in Begichevka and from there traveled about the countryside organizing soup kitchens with remarkable efficiency. Something had tapped his passionate, tireless nature, for he moved like a lion, back and forth from Yasnaya Polyana throughout the county, riding from one village to the next, sleeping in barren huts, spending hour after hour passing out grain and bread. He put his older sons and daughters to work too, and over a period of the next two years, Tolstoy oversaw the distribution of supplies, the gathering of firewood, and the establishment of 248 soup kitchens and feeding stations throughout the southern and central provinces.

When time could be found, he made notes and wrote articles about the famine. "Today is Sept. 15 [1892], from Yasnaya Polyana: It's two days since I returned from Begichevka, where I spent three good days. Wrote a draft report and conclusion. A depressingly painful impression made on me by a train full of officials and soldiers, going to put down a riot."[5] His pamphlets and letters on the subject of the famine and its causes (the government and the upper classes, of course) were widely read. Money was raised in England and France, bringing the famine to the attention of an entire continent. The government of Tsar Alexander III was furious, and Pobedonostsev, head of the Holy Synod, accused Tolstoy of trying to incite a peasant revolution. Tolstoy wrote on, worked on. The soup kitchens multiplied. In short, he had become a man of public action.

Consider for a moment the power he had accumulated, this man who detested any form of politics, this prophet who called for nonresistance and pacifism at all times. Even if he had remained a farmer and had never written a line, the ancient name of Tolstoy is woven clearly into Russian history. (His ancestor, Peter Andreyevich, served Peter the Great as minister of state.) But Leo Tolstoy wrote *War and Peace* and *Anna Karenina,* two of the greatest novels of the Western world. For the Russian people, writers such as Tolstoy possess unique status, both as guardians of truth and as creators of history and repositories of national conscience. His name and genius would have been enough to guarantee him permanent devotion, but after his religious crisis, Tolstoy's word commanded a different kind of attention—he asked a huge country to look again at those accepted truths and institutions which had ossified in place at the center of Russian life. How should we live, he asked. Are we our brother's keeper? Some attacked him. Others worshiped him. But he gained a moral authority well beyond that of any other writer.

And now, Tolstoy rolls up his sleeves and starts passing out bread to the hungry.

The government was decidedly ill at ease with Leo Tolstoy. After all, by questioning the church and its view of the sanctity of Christ, Tolstoy had challenged the divine right of the monarchy to rule, had he not? And now he was talking up the famine, focusing on the massive inequity that was at the heart of the Russian system. In their nervousness and imprecision the tsar's men called him an "Antichrist." Consideration was given, briefly, to confining him to a fortress for unruly clergy, which he probably would have loved. Completely ignoring government harassment and surveillance, Tolstoy continued to solicit monies and supplies to relieve the famine (in a rare moment of common purpose, Sonya and Chertkov both wrote appeals to foreign newspapers) and to press forward in explaining his creed of nonviolence, which he called nonresistance to evil.

We must conclude from reading his diary and letters that Tolstoy was not unhappy in the public fray. A few years earlier, he had expressed impatience with the written word. "There are too many books," he complained, "and the world will go on just the same whatever books are written nowadays. If Christ came and had the Gospels printed, ladies would try and get his autograph, and nothing more. We must stop writing, reading and talking; we must *act*."[6] He had acted, and the peasantry, the newspapers, his disciples, and official Russia were made witness.

By the fall of 1892, the work of the famine relief over, he returned to Yasnaya Polyana, to his own fields. Ilya Repin and N. N. Gay, the most prominent Russian portrait painters of their time, both visited Yasnaya Polyana. For the most part, "the seer of the flesh" enjoyed having his portrait painted. Among the many splendid results is the work entitled *Tolstoy Ploughing*. Repin gave the world a perfect painting of the master to accompany the multitude of words. Tolstoy's brow is furrowed, his shoulders hunched over the plough, the earth is brown and fertile beneath him, his dress is that of a peasant. His internal conflicts are not revealed in this painting, nor is his distinctly troubled marriage. He is ploughing, and now the world was watching.

Little Vanichka, the thirteenth and last of the Tolstoy children, had an air of such enchantment and promise about him that many felt this boy alone seemed to possess some of Tolstoy's sensibility and, perhaps, genius. Sonya

Sonya, with a portrait of Vanichka, soon after his death.

adored him. She tended to him minutely, as she had most of her children, but he elicited in her, as in his brothers and sisters, a particular passion. Alexandra suggested that he had unusual intuition and a keen sense of the larger world. A famous scientist visiting the family in Moscow said, "The first I set eyes on that child, I knew he must either die a premature death or become a greater genius than his father."[7]

On February 21, 1895, just short of his seventh birthday, Vanichka died of meningitis. He had complained of fever and the doctor was called, but in thirty-six hours the child was dead. Sonya's sobs of anguish carried through the house and were felt in the bones of a stricken family. She held Vanichka's cold head in her hands. Alexandra, his closest companion, cowered in her room, and Leo Tolstoy was "nearly unconscious with sorrow." Later he wrote: "The death of Vanichka was for me, like the death of Nikolenka*—no to a far greater degree—a manifestation of God, a drawing of me towards Him."

*His older brother.

Somewhat morbidly, he added, "Yes, one must always live as if a favorite child is dying in a room nearby. He is always dying. And I am always dying."[8] He noted in a letter: "I have never felt in Sonya or myself such a need for love and such an aversion toward all disunity and evil. I have never loved Sonya as much as I do now."[9] Death had united them, however temporarily, in a way that life could not.

The effect on Sonya of the death of this last beloved child was complex. Her husband could turn to God—his God—and could go back to his writing ("I feel like writing something literary," he recorded three weeks later), could go out and ride his bicycle, which he did. She walked about the house clinging to the child's toys. How could she still be on earth, and he not? She sought consolation in prayer. But in fact Sonya did not have Tolstoy's spiritual resources. Nor his intellectual resources. She was above all a mother, mother of many, mother of them all, mother of Yasnaya Polyana, mother of Vanichka, of whom she said, "He saved me from evil. Mine is a bad and harsh nature; he softened it by his love."[10]

Hers was not a bad and harsh nature, but she could be suffocatingly possessive and self-dramatizing. As a young married woman, her psychological life was rich with sensitive, delicate feelings, many of which she confided to her diary. Two decades later, burdened by almost constant pregnancies and infinite worry, something of her kinder nature seemed to give way. Her inborn jealousy, with much to contest it, grew out of control. She could, at times, become vindictive, and was prone to hysterics. The death of Vanichka seemed to release these qualities in her with additional force. To Alexandra, a child with whom she was to have a dire struggle in later life, she is reported to have said, "Why did it have to be him? Why couldn't it be you?"

Sonya was no longer young, and the year after Vanichka's death she developed what can only be described as a schoolgirl crush on a rather pudgy pianist-composer named Taneyev, whom Tolstoy came to detest. That his music brought her comfort cannot be questioned. That he seemed to be able to give her "A rich, joyful gift" seems harder to believe, since Taneyev is not known to have uttered one memorable word, or done anything except play the piano. He was ordinary and probably uninterested in women. When she invited him to spend the summer at Yasnaya Polyana, Sonya was inviting real trouble, for Tolstoy, returned to his earlier longing to leave his wife and their gentry life, began to consider really doing so. He wrote letters of farewell. The longest of these, dated July 18, 1897, is an earnest, surely sincere assessment of his perpetual conflict about life at Yasnaya Polyana:

I have long been troubled by the inconsistency between my life and my convictions. I could not make you change your life and the habits in which I had trained you, and until now I have felt equally unable to go away and leave you, lest in so doing I should deprive the children, whilst still young, of such influence, even if slight, which I could still have upon them, and also lest I should cause you all grief. But I can no longer continue living as I have lived for sixteen years, sometimes struggling against and irritating you, sometimes succumbing to the familiar temptations that surround me all the time; and now I have decided to do what I have long wished to do—to go away.

First, because this life is becoming more and more of a burden to me, as my years increase, I long more and more for solitude; and second, because now that the children are grown up, my influence is no longer needed in the house, and all of you have more vital interests which will make you feel my absence less. But the principal thing is that just as the Hindus, when they approach their sixtieth year, retire to the woods, just as any aged and religious man wishes to devote his last years to God and not to jokes, gossip and tennis, so I, having entered my seventieth year, long with my whole soul for peace, solitude, and, if not complete harmony, then at least not such flagrant discord between my life and my conscience and convictions.

If I were to carry out my plan openly, there would be entreaties, reproaches, arguments and complaints, and I might weaken and perhaps not carry out my intention—and yet it must be carried out. Therefore please forgive me if my action hurts you, forgive me, all of you, in your hearts; but chiefly you, Sonya; let me go with good will; do not search for me, do not complain and do not condemn me.

That I leave you does not prove that I am dissatisfied with you, I know that you were unable, literally unable, and are still unable, to see and feel as I do, and therefore that you could not and cannot change your life and make sacrifices for the sake of something of which you are not conscious. Therefore, I do not blame you, but on the contrary, remember with love and gratitude the thirty-five years of our life together, especially the first half of that period when, with the motherly self-sacrifice which is innate in you, you bore so energetically and firmly what you considered to be your duty . . .[11]

This was not the first of such farewell letters to Sonya. She had received them before and was utterly terrified of his acting on the threat to leave. Earlier letters were more damning; this one had a lofty, resigned tone. At this point, his communications to her suggest the thinking of an essentially selfish man, one who valued his own purity of thought above the welfare of those near to him. He had switched gears on them, become a saint, and moved into another way of seeing the world, particularly the world of Yasnaya Polyana. Sonya was an entrenched follower of the old order. For a woman nourished on the idea that God meant them to hold onto their property, following the simple life was clearly not to be.

Equally clear is the fact that life at Yasnaya Polyana really was quite painful for him. The frivolities aside (tennis, gossip), he was still surrounded with servants, and though he professed not to be able to stand being waited on, they were still there. To be sure, he cleaned his own room, but the household staff roamed about, charged with the traditional job of cleaning up after others. Servants in white gloves still served dinner. Isolated within what had been his own house, he simply did not have the will or the ability to transform the world of Yasnaya Polyana.

What could he do? Many of his followers had established farming communities in which everyone held an equal rank and lofty ideals. But that does not appear to be what he himself was seeking; Tolstoy was really far too much of an egotist, too much of an individual to blend into the communal mold. He wanted to "retire to the woods and devote his life to God." Just Tolstoy and God.

The question can be asked, Why didn't he retire to the woods? Chertkov, in a much later book, suggests that for Tolstoy the ultimate Christian sacrifice was to remain at home, to remain in the hedonistic lair of Yasnaya Polyana to help steady that ship and endure its indignities. Was a compromise possible? He had from time to time spoken to one of his favorite peasants of his wish to leave home. Could he not have found the peace and solitude in a rudimentary hut near the village of Yasnaya Polyana, close to the peasants whom he so re-

Family group.

vered, where in the event of inevitable family crisis he could be consulted but was out of harm's way (Sonya's way) most of the time? No, such a thought is too practical for a sweeping mind such as Tolstoy's. He continued to defer solution, as he hesitated to (and finally did not) deliver the letter to Sonya.

In this missive to his wife he does not yet use the word *escape*—it figures in his later correspondence. Therefore, we could conclude that although life at Yasnaya Polyana had become contradictory and difficult, it was not yet unbearable; there were moments for the hedonist in Tolstoy to find deep pleasure in the gathering of mushrooms, evenings at the piano with the children, walks in his beloved lime grove, or a horseback ride through his own forests. There were pleasant moments with Sonya. He was torn, was still very bound to her. "I teach others but do not know how to live myself," Tolstoy wrote to Chertkov, which suggested that he understood the nature and magnitude of his inner struggle.[12]

Something that he did not appear to understand is his wife. To suggest that she would let him go with goodwill, not search for him, "do not complain and do not condemn me," is a wild miscalculation. But perhaps he can be forgiven, for this letter was written in 1897. The nature and depth of their animosity had miles to go.

Resurrection. Even the title sounds vast and forbidding. Tolstoy began this, his third big novel, in 1895 and finished it four years later. In *Resurrection,* his guns are now turned against Russian institutions—the courts, the prison system, the bureaucracy—all of which, he contends, turn men into monsters. It was new territory for him, and for the most part *Resurrection* is a powerful work. It does not, however, stand in the same category as *War and Peace* and *Anna Karenina,* for the principal characters, Prince Nekhludov and the prostitute Maslova, lack the shading and depth of feeling found in Anna, Pierre, and Natasha.

How can an individual redeem acts of injustice? In a moment of youthful passion, Nekhludov has made Maslova, a servant girl, pregnant; he abandons her, the child is born dead, she becomes a prostitute. He finds her years later in a courtroom, on trial for murder, and decides to spend the rest of his life redressing his earlier injustice to her. Nekhludov and Maslova make their way in a somewhat wooden manner through the book, stopping for bursts of propaganda and predictable reflection. Yet *Resurrection,* the lesser of the big novels, made a huge impression in Europe and America. It was, by the end of the nineteenth century, more widely read than either of the other two masterpieces.

In this book Tolstoy mocks the rituals of the Orthodox church with extra vengeance. Provocative it surely was. The censor stripped away at much of the book, officials fumed, but the Russian reading public was mesmerized by *Resurrection.* In addition to the attack on the church, the book remorselessly unmasked some of the suffocating institutions of Russian life, of which a growing number of the population was beginning to feel suspicious and bitter. *Resurrection* was compared in its time to Victor Hugo's *Les Misérables.* It sparked debate and controversy, giving Tolstoy something which he didn't really need: additional notoriety and power.

The writing of *Resurrection* was hastened, encouraged in its pace, by a strange source: a religious sect named the Dukhobors, whose beliefs coincided somewhat with Tolstoy's, particularly in their creed of nonviolence. This large (ten thousand) group of what was called "spirit wrestlers" lived in communes and refused to serve in the army. The Dukhobors had been banished to the Caucasus, where they fared rather badly, and to give vivid demonstration of their most cherished belief, that of the refusal to bear arms, the sect held a sort of powwow in which they burned all of their swords and guns while singing hymns around the crackling bonfire. Cossack soldiers, lying in wait, attacked their camp and beat them mercilessly. Most of the land held by the Dukhobors was then confiscated, and they were simply left to scatter and, presumably, to die. Tolstoy was horrified and threw himself into their defense.

His strongest weapon had always been his pen. Now, what about the rewards from his pen? If the proceeds from *Resurrection* could be spent to help the besieged Dukhobors, they would be spared certain death. This sweeping charity would justify the sale of the work and its speedy completion.

On this one even Sonya agreed, and Chertkov was absolutely elated. They succeeded in arousing public concern for the Dukhobors in England by endorsing an article called, plainly, *The Persecution of the Christians in Russia in 1895,* and then Tolstoy published in Russia a piece entitled *Give Help*. This pamphlet was mailed directly to the tsar. The government of Nicholas II was enraged. How could they stop him? How could they discredit him?

They couldn't. By 1897 the moral position of Tolstoy in the world was such that to confine him in any way or to exile him would add the component of martyrdom to his growing public stature. The tsar and his men were frustrated. What is a poor monarch to do when faced with such opposition?

The response of Pobedonostsev, head of the Holy Synod, and the monarchy was considered pale but mean. In February of 1897 they exiled Chertkov to England; a small number of Tolstoy's less powerful disciples were scattered into rural Russia. If the government couldn't get at him, they would punish his friends. This exiling of Tolstoy's partisans caused contempt and indignation through the circles of "advanced thinkers" in St. Petersburg. Tolstoy's support increased, as did his vigor. In a letter he wrote: "The sad thing is that they won't lay a finger on me. They are defeating their purpose however, for by leaving me free to speak the truth, they are compelling me to speak. And I have the impression that much remains to be said." As to Chertkov, Tolstoy was perhaps even more comfortable writing to him than having his austere presence at hand. In their lifetime, these men exchanged over one thousand letters. During this period, their dialogue was sometimes argumentative, but for the most part intense and often rhapsodic. Tolstoy noted that Chertkov was "so full of light, so happy and simple. What is going on inside is far more important than an enforced change of residence."[13]

In 1898 and 1899, the Dukhobors were allowed to leave for Canada, their passage paid for in large part by the sale of *Resurrection* (80,000 roubles, worth about $225,000 at that time). Despite his inner conflict about the *use*

Tolstoy and Chertkov in his second-floor study.

of money and the dubious role of charity, Tolstoy could not have helped but feel some satisfaction. Though his partisans might be scattered, he was still in Russia, at Yasnaya Polyana, his voice at the center of dissent. The meridian of moral force, said one supporter, went right through his living room.

Another kind of dissent, Yasnaya Polyana, July 16, 1897: "Masha got married and I was sorry for her, as one is sorry for a thoroughbred horse that is made to cart water. What will come of it I can't imagine," Tolstoy wrote, perhaps more sorry for himself than for his daughter, for Masha had been his favorite and his truest believer.[14] Now she was fleeing—and her choice for a husband was just exactly the kind of feckless young nobleman about whom Tolstoy had been scornful for years. Actually, Masha had married her cousin, Prince Nikolai Obolensky, the grandson of Leo Tolstoy's sister, Marya. And the next year, Tanya, at thirty-five, married a widower, a father of six; she took herself off to live on his estate at Kochety. "Tanya worries me with her frivolity,"

Tolstoy playing the piano with Alexandra.

Tolstoy noted. "She has withdrawn into egotistical love."[15] His devoted daughters were leaving him, and he was none too nice about it. There are very few references in his letters or diaries to the possibility of their own happiness, these two lonely older daughters of his. "All their weaknesses are understandable and touching," he wrote with resignation.[16] Of the weakness, one can assume he means their desertion of his household. All of his daughters were deeply, perhaps disturbingly, attached to him; that two out of the three of them managed to marry was a triumph.

Difficult as it might have been to be a Tolstoy daughter, it was no easier to be his son. He clearly couldn't stand the younger ones, Misha and Andrei, who were pretty much lined up with their mother anyway. Lev, talented and nervous, was an unsteady figure who suffered terribly from having such an overpowering father. Ilya, the sensual youth, the sportsman, married early and found little to do. Of the sons, it was perhaps Sergei, the oldest, who managed to actually please his father. He developed an active interest in music, and like his sister Tanya, to whom he was close in age, he managed to maintain a dialogue with both of his parents when their quarrels divided the household.

In 1899, he accompanied the Dukhobors to Canada to help them resettle. "Seryozha [Sergei] is very close to me in deed and feeling. I deliberately don't provoke him with words," wrote Tolstoy.[17] Certainly those of his children who could join their father *in deeds* were far more likely to find him respectful and affectionate. And no one had come closer to him in deeds and feeling than Masha, who used to plough the fields, dress like a peasant, and tend to the sick. But then she up and married a foppish prince.

If Tolstoy was recalcitrant with his children, he was charm itself to visitors. He notes "a whole host of guests" that summer of '97. Among them, a sprightly American chemist and nutritionist named Wilbur Atwater, who, encouraged by Jane Addams of Hull House (who had been there the year before), decided to call at Yasnaya Polyana one day in September. A few days later, he reported on his visit in a letter to his granddaughter:

"The grounds were not well kept at all, . . . and the furniture was very plain indeed. The walls were hung with portraits of the former generations of Tolstoys. The members of the family came in and went out entirely without ceremony. There were no formal introductions. I was treated exactly as if I'd been there for months."

And as to his talk with Tolstoy, Atwater wrote, "He gave me some of his ideas in a general way and began to criticize the present course of scientific research, saying that not enough attention was given to things connected with the daily life of the people . . . Of course I could not argue with him, and told him so very frankly. He replied with equal frankness and the greatest kindness. As he talked of his ideas, generally in French though sometimes in German or English, I would repeat it in English, using my own paraphrases, to bring out my idea of his meaning. He would correct me if I didn't get it right. And in that way I thought I got at his spirit very well."

Such charm in the informality of the family! Such elegance in the exchange of thought and language, only to be interrupted as the bell for nine o'clock tea rang. Later, as Atwater bid his host good-bye, "he assured me in such a way that I could not doubt sincerity, that the conversation had been to him also a source of real satisfaction."

Real satisfaction was a rarity in these later Tolstoy years. It seems to have been possible in occasional meetings with intelligent, nonargumentative visitors. In Wilbur Atwater's letter to his granddaughter, he suggests that "he [Tolstoy] is a man with whom even the absolutely autocratic Russian government has to count most carefully."[18]

The absolutely autocratic government was now led by young Tsar Nicholas II. A man of affable nature, more worldly than his father, Tsar Alexander III, he ruled by divine right over 120 million people, over territory comprising almost one-sixth of the earth. However, he proved to be as obdurate as his father on matters concerning the monarchy; in 1895, the year after his accession, Nicholas dismissed the idea of constitutional government as "senseless dreams." As the forces of reform and revolution quickened their pace, he remained blind to both the circumstances and the need for change. A man devoted to family values and particularly to his wife, the German-born Empress Alexandra, Tsar Nicholas II seemed more comfortable in the bosom of his family than as the leader of a massive nation. He took counsel from the grand dukes, his conservative uncles, and the continually reactionary Pobedonostsev, Procurator of the Holy Synod.

Possibly it was Tolstoy's growing influence within Russia, or perhaps those energetically anti-church scenes in *Resurrection,* which served to goad Pobedonostsev and the hierarchy of the church into action. They had certainly

Sonya photographed at Yasnaya Polyana in 1896.

been frustrated by him for a long time. On February 22, 1901, the Holy Synod met and issued a decree which formally excommunicated Leo Tolstoy from the Russian Orthodox church.

"God has permitted a false prophet to appear in our midst," read the announcement. "A world famous author, Russian by birth, Orthodox by baptism and education, Count Tolstoy, led astray by pride, has boldly and insolently dared to oppose God, Christ and his holy heirs . . . The Church no longer recognizes him among her children and cannot do so until he has repented . . ."

Repent? They knew him not. On the contrary, Tolstoy seemed pleased. He absorbed his excommunication good-naturedly, noting that although the church hierarchy seemed ready to brave the gates of hell, they seemed to "tremble before a retired lieutenant of artillery."

Sonya, happy for a chance to take a public position in his defense, fired off an articulate and impassioned letter of protest to the head of the church in

Tolstoy on his favorite horse, Delire.

St. Petersburg. This letter, thanks to the network of supporters within and outside of Russia, was widely reprinted. In Moscow, where Tolstoy had gone for a doctor's appointment, the excommunicant now found himself surrounded with joyous throngs. Ovations in the street! Groups of students followed him, cheering, and soon crowds swelled to the point where mounted police had to be brought in to protect him from his admirers. "Hurrah Tolstoy! Long life to Tolstoy!" they called as he nervously acknowledged their cheers. Teatralny Square was jammed with people "shouting and waving their hats and expressing their enthusiasm in every extravagant manner."[19] At home, telegrams and letters of concern piled up. Visitors streamed in night and day, and a festive atmosphere prevailed. A few weeks later, Tolstoy drafted a simple, unflinching response to the Holy Synod, in which he restated his creed. Again he accused the church of misusing the word of Christ. His letter, reprinted by hand, was read by an eager public.

In Russia and on the Continent, many were moved by the excommunication of Tolstoy. The following irreverent observation by the critic and

Tolstoy and granddaughter Tanya.

newspaper director Alexis Suvorin hints at the complexity of the times:

"We have two tsars, Nicholas II and Leo Tolstoy," he noted in his diary. "Which is the stronger? Nicholas II is powerless against Tolstoy, and cannot make him tremble on his throne, whereas Tolstoy is incontestably shaking the throne of Nicholas II and his whole dynasty. He is anathmatized, the Synod publishes a decree against him. Tolstoy replies and his reply circulates in handwritten copies and in the foreign press. Let anyone lift a finger against Tolstoy and the whole world will be up in arms and our administration will turn tail and run."[20]

Such was the power of Leo Tolstoy in May of 1901.

7

FLIGHT
[1901–1910]

After the Ball is a short story about Russia. Tolstoy wrote it at Yasnaya Polyana in 1903. "It was a delightful ball," he wrote. "It was a splendid room, with a gallery for the orchestra, which was famous at the time, and consisted of serfs belonging to a musical landowner. The refreshments were magnificent and the champagne flowed in rivers." *After the Ball** is a small masterpiece and a testament to Tolstoy's mature genius. After continual absorption with moral writings, letters, appeals, and articles, his passion and sensibility was still alert to the working of fiction.

At a provincial ball, a handsome, aging colonel dances gracefully with his daughter. The young narrator, Ivan Vasileivich, notes with "enraptured sympathy" the older man's gentleness, elegance of bearing, and the delicate steps with which he and his daughter Varinka circle the room. After the ball—that is, at sunrise the next morning—Ivan Vasileivich, by now in love with Varinka, walks to her house, perhaps to catch a glimpse of her. Instead, to his horror, he sees her father, the graceful old colonel of the night before, directing his troops as they administer a savage beating to a Tartar soldier who had attempted to desert. Varinka's father, with his rosy face and white mustache, furiously encourages the other soldiers to strike harder, as the poor

---

* In the early edition, the story is called *After the Dance*.

Tartar, who had begged for mercy, is by now "something so many-coloured, wet, red, and unnatural, that one could hardly believe it was a human being."

"Bring new sticks!" demands the colonel, as the beating goes on. And this is the same man who danced with such grace and civility the evening before!

The colonel is the symbolic product of Mother Russia, whose people at once tenderly worship icons and feel the delicate verses of Pushkin in their veins, and yet who are also capable of legendary and sustained brutality against their own people. Thus it had been, through the mercilessness of Ivan the Terrible, and would continue into the twentieth century under the purges of Stalin and life in the Gulags, as recorded by Solzhenitsyn. For anyone asking why, Tolstoy's story gives an exacting picture of the contradictory nature of Russia and her people.

Tolstoy the storyteller was flourishing again—his most perfect genius for expressing a sensory feeling, the quality of a moment, the essence of things, was very much intact. *Hajid Murat* and *Father Sergius,* both major works of fiction, were still to come. Tolstoy was seventy-five. A year earlier he had spent months in the Crimea, fighting off two dangerous illnesses, angina pectoris and influenza. But he wasn't done for yet. Tolstoy spent the next five years exclusively at Yasnaya Polyana. He rode his horse every day.

1907. Yasnaya Polyana. An incident occurred which seemed to polarize Tolstoy and his wife, perhaps irrevocably.

Neighboring peasants were caught stealing timber from the woods and cabbages from the garden. Estate vandalism was an old story, but in recent months there had been an increase of incidents throughout the province. At Yasnaya Polyana, the bailiff scared the peasants off with a few gunshots.

Tolstoy had long accepted these light misdemeanors as unimportant, but Sonya was enraged. Encouraged by her son Andrei, she asked the governor of Tula* for guards, for officials to police the estate against peasant vandals. This meant that the house of the great proponent of nonviolence, the estate of the man who regarded the ownership of property as evil, was now under uniformed protection. Tolstoy's critics, and there were many, had a field day.

To make things worse, the policemen sent to offer this protection then raided the village of Yasnaya Polyana and made four arrests. Peasants arrested

* Andrei, always something of a loose cannon, had run off the year before with the wife of the governor of Tula.

Portrait of Tolstoy in 1909.

and imprisoned for cutting trees and filching cabbages! Tolstoy begged his wife to call off the prosecutions. She refused, reminding him that there had been a fire set on a neighboring estate. The guards would stay. What horror he must have felt at the presence of police, seven in number, roaming the property with guns, prepared to render violence. Tolstoy described the situation as "pure hell."

When the governor of Tula, under whose supervision this sweep of the village and subsequent arrests took place, kept his troops at Yasnaya Polyana, he did so at the request of the authority at hand—Countess Tolstoy. For it was she to whom the legal authority at Yasnaya Polyana had been passed, and at this point Count Tolstoy was but an anguished onlooker. In his diary, Tolstoy records his "depressed state of mind."

To try to put an end to this charade, he enlisted the support of Alexandra, his most vehemently faithful daughter, who, as was her nature, threw herself into the task. "I implored mother to send the guards away," she wrote.

"I quarreled with her, with my brother Andrei, I lost my temper, I wept. It was unbearable to see Father suffering. Finally I went to the Governor with a letter from Father, begging him to free the peasants who had been arrested, but his curt reply was: 'Your mother Countess Tolstoy requested me to undertake the protection of Yasnaya Polyana and of your family and I am merely carrying out her request.' "[1]

The guards stayed on for two years.

Again, as he often had since 1884, Tolstoy wrote of his wish to take flight, to escape, to leave Yasnaya Polyana, the scene of this indignity. But he didn't do it, citing as reason that he didn't wish to bring wild unhappiness to Sonya, "who is only convinced she is doing her duty." A reading of his diaries would suggest that he was also somewhat afraid of her. Sonya could be vindictive and her moods were erratic. Tolstoy's notes during this period find frequent reference to his feeling "physically weak," and one senses his inability to cope with Sonya. The year before, they had been united, however briefly, by yet again another death: Beloved Masha, at age thirty-five, died of inflam-

Tolstoy with Alexandra,
1908.

mation of the lungs. But as with other periods of grief, their sense of sympathy and goodwill toward each other didn't last. "Sonya came in and we started talking about the wood, about people stealing, and about the children selling things at half price, and I couldn't suppress my anger," he records in April of 1907 in his diary, and pleads, "Lord, Help me. Help me."[2]

The incident surrounding the arrest of the peasants had the effect of solidifying the antagonism between Alexandra and Sonya. Now she, Alexandra, the third daughter, announced that she would never marry, that she would forever be her father's disciple; thus she began to take Sonya's place at Leo Tolstoy's side. Alexandra now copied his manuscripts, managed his correspondence, and sat next to him at the piano. And he regarded her as his principal defender. That is, until his other principal defender came back from exile.

When Chertkov returned to Russia from England in 1907, his native country was in a very confused and dismal state. The Russo-Japanese War had been lost, and famine, again, was on the rampage, urban poverty more widespread and painful than ever. After a costly political struggle and a massive general strike in October of 1905, the Tsar was forced to allow the beginnings of constitutional government: freedom of the press and an elected parliament, called the duma. This frail assembly proved more symbolic than real in terms of power, but the duma did include some peasants—and a hint, poorly understood, of things to come. Tolstoy, the purist, believed that no political reform was of any consequence without spiritual reform, so he had little warmth for the duma. He had lost some support in the country because of his fixed stand on pacifism and on neutrality in the Russo-Japanese War. "—I am neither for or against the Japanese or Russia, I am only for the working classes of both countries," he announced to a nation not used to losing wars to Orientals.

Tolstoy remained contemptuous of the new political changes, but then again he had always resisted any form of institutional authority, even when the sands shifted toward popular representation. Though love for him throughout Russia might have eroded slightly during this period, the worshipful population at Yasnaya Polyana, the "dark ones," groups of ragged Tolstoyans and petitioners, increased in number. In fact, Yasnaya Polyana had developed something of a circus atmosphere.

"Neighbors from among the 'dark people' came every evening to settle themselves in a semicircle around Father, expecting him to say something,"

Alexandra records.[3] He was besieged by supplicants requesting money, nervous landowners asking if owning private property really was a sin, students, vegetarians, those lost in love, lunatics, and the curious—many just wished to sit at Tolstoy's feet. Friends—Orlov, a painter, and the pianist Goldenweiser— settled in near Yasnaya Polyana; the estate had become their Mecca. Sonya, understandably, felt put upon. There were sometimes thirty for lunch. The word *privacy* has no direct translation in the Russian language. It had little applicability in the mayhem at Yasnaya Polyana—except when Tolstoy was in his study, at work on his writings.

Into this atmosphere strode Chertkov, accompanied by his pencil-thin, sickly wife, Galya, who, Alexandra records, gave her the shivers. In exile, Chertkov had been productive, publishing and circulating Tolstoy's writings. The guardian of Tolstoy's word now seemed prepared to take over his life. Chertkov had always been a handsome, humorless man, but he appeared to have grown physically more overbearing during his years in England.

In a dictatorial manner, he edited the Master's word. He installed a secretary of his own choosing, N. N. Gusev, whose job it was to supervise Tolstoy's massive correspondence. No one heretofore had been permitted into Tolstoy's study during the midday hours when he was working. Chertkov barreled in. Sonya renewed her dislike of him instantly and was perplexed to find that Chertkov seemed to be removing manuscripts from Yasnaya Polyana in large number. Her jealousy, her darkest and most active demon, was aroused as Tolstoy spent hours with his devoted partisan. She noted in her diary that Chertkov was "practically living at our house."

Actually, Chertkov built himself a good-sized house of his own just three miles from Yasnaya Polyana, at Telyatinki. Although he was quick to urge Tolstoy to give up *his* worldly goods, Chertkov, with an inherited income of 20,000 roubles a year, did not feel that renunciations applied to him. Here, at Telyatinki, he planned to establish the headquarters for the New Christianity, based on Tolstoy's writings. Alexandra, from whom he bought the property, describes the main house as "large, with two stories, built on a corridor scheme like a hotel. Only the rooms in the right and left wings were a little cozier, with verandahs and Italian windows. They were for Chertkov's mother and for his wife. The 'helpers'* were to live in the upper story. There was also a large hall for gatherings, theatricals, and lectures . . . Father walked about without saying anything. When we came out into the yard he said to me, 'It's

* Tolstoyans who served as Chertkov's secretaries.

sad . . . It pains me to see Chertkov build such a large, luxurious house.' "[4]

If Tolstoy was sad, it was only fleetingly, for his spirits rose at the return home of his arch-disciple. He seemed energized and, more than ever, dependent upon their "joyous communion." Under Chertkov's eye, Tolstoy's moral writings and essays continued to pour forth. The mail and newspaper reports from the countryside as well as from Moscow brought to Yasnaya Polyana fresh stories of hangings—official and unofficial—terrorism, and brutality; a report of twenty peasants hanged for robbing a landowner's estate moved Tolstoy to fury as well as to tears.

Thus he wrote the fervent and eloquent article *I Cannot Be Silent,* his most passionate work against capital punishment, revealing anew his genuine anguish at man's inhumanity to man. Newspaper editors who printed excerpts from the article were arrested, yet the informal network that served to distribute Tolstoy's moral writings was well practiced. Mimeographed or hand-copied, *I Cannot Be Silent* circulated throughout Russia and in most countries of Europe throughout the year 1908.

Russian society at this point was facing the prospect of genuine disintegration. The ball, of *After the Ball,* was soon to disappear from sight, and the gentry, particularly the landed gentry, felt deeply threatened by the forces of an angry peasantry and restless proletariat. The monarchy was weakened, and life was unbearably harsh for most of Russia's 100 million peasants. Lenin, in exile, was biding his time.

By August of 1908, Yasnaya Polyana and its inhabitants were bent in preparation for Tolstoy's eightieth birthday celebration. A jubilee committee was formed, Sonya composed a statement, schoolchildren sang, presents arrived, telegrams poured in, and Tolstoy wrote a friend, "Do what you can to put an end to this jubilee and liberate me," but it was not to be. The event went off. Tolstoy managed to be fairly gracious, and the nation seemed pleased for the chance to pause for a few days from the contentious atmosphere of the moment to honor him. Among his early presents came a strange-looking apparition from America:

"Father received a present of a sort we had never seen before—a Dictaphone sent to him from America by Thomas Edison," Alexandra tells us. "When I had it set up, he tried to speak into it, but was so excited that he stuttered and forgot what he intended to say. 'Stop the machine, stop it,' he cried to me. 'It is dreadfully exciting,' he added with a sigh. 'Probably such a machine is good for well-balanced Americans but not for us Russians.' "[5]

During that period the household of Yasnaya Polyana received another American gift—a Remington typewriter. This one was more of a success, perhaps not so dreadfully exciting but for a man with his voluminous correspondence, quite a godsend. Tanya learned the keyboard first, but it was Alexandra who seemed to take to it. The study in which it was placed came to be known as the Remington Room. "Progress," or the fruits of it, for a man who once declared the railroad to be unnecessary, had its day.

Within the grounds of Yasnaya Polyana, the balance was shifting decisively away from that which was familial and intimate. In the physical sense, little had changed on the estate since the early days of Tolstoy's marriage. The eye still took comfort in the stability of the white gateposts at the entrance, visitors could feel the comfort of cool birch trees lining the *prospekt,* the same bathing house still jutted out over the bend in the Voronka River, Tolstoy's apple orchard was resplendent—everything was in place, suspended above time. Yet the sense of insularity, the feeling of Yasnaya Polyana as a world of its own, self-sustaining—this exquisite isolation was drawing to a close. Trains to and from Tula were numerous. The mails brought in correspondence from all over the world—from Gandhi, George Bernard Shaw, H. G. Wells, Ernest Crosby, Tomas Masaryk. The international press had discovered Yasnaya Polyana and its prophet, and they flocked to interview him.

And into a place which had its share of visitors, another category was added: the cosmopolitan, high-minded, well-placed visitor, many from America, who arrived in an endless stream, often unannounced. People like William Jennings Bryan, Jane Addams, and Wilbur Atwater—intelligent, curious folk who wished to talk with Tolstoy, have a chat about his ideas that they might take home an impression of him. He found these interviews exhausting. Where were the "gentle caresses of the old house" Tolstoy had referred to as a young man? Gone. Yasnaya Polyana had become a shrine.

Yet not every voice was worshipful:

"Are you still alive, you old swine?"

Could these words, addressed to the master, be coming from the peasants of Yasnaya Polyana?

While out riding in his forest—and he liked to ride alone—Tolstoy came upon a group of peasants looking for wood. "Hasn't the devil got you yet? You might have died long ago," they called to him.[6] Imagine Tolstoy's anguish; he well might have wished he had died long ago. Goaded by Sonya's unwillingness to rent them forest land or sell them timber, encouraged by the church to think of Tolstoy as a heretic, small groups of peasants occasionally vented their anger at the man who was considered to be their champion. From that moment on, Sonya insisted that either Alexandra or Tolstoy's doctor, Dushan Makovitsky, ride with him.

How things had changed in the seventy years or so that had passed since young Lev had curled up in his grandmother's room to be lulled asleep by the blind storyteller ("There once was a king and he had one son . . ."). Now the authority of Nicholas II was eroding, the balance of power was shifting. Peasant violence, murder, burning of houses and barns was frequent throughout the countryside of Tula. No more the sense that the master and peasants were all woven together by history and the common bonds of the property itself. It was 1908, and the era of idle afternoons and gentle evenings of cards and a little piano music was soon to be directly challenged. The Bolshevik Revolution was nine years away.

Yasnaya Polyana, home of the great rural philosopher, was now seen in a different light by the outside world, for it had become, in essence, a public place. Alexandra recalls: "We were deprived of the common human satisfaction of living unobserved by outsiders, of talking nonsense, joking, singing, being ourselves, since we knew that every word and act was being immediately fixed on paper."[7]

Everyone now had a claim on Yasnaya Polyana. Tolstoyans and peasant sectarians—in fact anyone who shared Tolstoy's views—believed that they should have access to him and to his house. No serious journalist felt complete without an audience with Tolstoy. Intellectuals saw the estate and its prophet as the font of wisdom (or argument). Painters painted him in every pose, in the fields, at his desk. Fleets of secretaries and typists took notes and kept diaries. Permanent hangers-on, like the sainted follower Marya Alexandrovna Schmidt, wanted to live near him, and moved into an outbuilding on the estate.

And fresh from his exile, redoubled in his purpose and energy, Chertkov also claimed a daily visit.

Between 1909 and 1910 Tolstoy had suffered two or three fainting spells, followed by memory loss. "Blood rushing away from the brain," in his doctor's terminology; perhaps he had a series of small strokes. He was eighty-two. Sonya, now sixty-six, had survived a major operation for the removal of a tumor. She now seemed possessed by boundless, almost kinetic, energy. She busied herself frantically, with copying, hours of repetitious piano playing, photography (a new hobby), and caring, minutely, for him. "It was mother's conviction that her principal task in life was to take care of father," Alexandra tells us. "Suffering from the inner discord between him and herself, she emphasized the external care for his well being. She was proud of the cap she had knitted for him, the blouse which she had neatly cut and sewn for him with her own hands. Thus she comforted herself, failing to understand that no care could atone for father's moral sufferings. She sincerely believed that father would be lost if she did not pour some meat broth into his vegetable soup . . ."[8] Thus she saw her role as his devoted life companion, his foremost guardian.

Now it was Chertkov who asked for, and received, Tolstoy's every confidence.

One might ask, What did Chertkov want? Simply put, he saw himself as the principal spokesman for Tolstoy's New Christianity, perhaps an heir apparent. Consistent with what he felt Tolstoy's moral obligation to be, he wanted the copyrights to *all* of Tolstoy's works, including the giant *War and Peace* (presently held by Sonya), placed in public domain, with all manuscripts kept in his, Chertkov's, care and, therefore, in the metaphoric sense, in his control.

Now that is not, of course, what he said. To queries, he would reply that he was Tolstoy's closest friend (perhaps this was true) and that he only wished to protect the Master from those who did not understand him. In addition to being manipulative, Chertkov possessed a kind of bloodless intelligence, a righteous determination, and a natural authority, to which Tolstoy gave in more often than one would suspect. Many of Tolstoy's old friends were wary of Chertkov. Aylmer Maude wrote of him: "I never knew anyone with such a capacity for enforcing his will on others. Everybody connected with him became his instrument, quarrelled with him, or had to escape. To resist him was difficult. It was fortunate that he cherished non resistant principles, for his physical as well as mental powers were redoubtable. But discarding physical violence seemed to leave him freer to employ mental coercion, and he was expert at its use."[9] The ultimate destruction rendered by Chertkov was this: He was willing to sacrifice the peace of mind of both Tolstoy and Sonya, at the end of their lives, on the altar of his pious, over-determined Christianity.

Yet, Chertkov was what might be called today a "cool hand." His voice was calm, in what was often a shrill atmosphere. He made clean, if reprehen-

Tolstoy and Sonya, in 1895.

sible, decisions. He joined with Tolstoy and talked for hours on end with him about the great issues that troubled them both. At all times, he kept his head.

Poor, poor Sonya did not. Predisposed from the early days to hysterics and possessiveness, she operated on the edge of emotional extremes. She felt, and indeed was, isolated within her household. Tolstoy had his supporters and the devotion of Alexandra. Except for occasional visits from the volatile Andrei, Sonya really had no one. Although she tried to rein in her strident outbursts, and her diary often touchingly reflects that struggle, she did not succeed. When Tolstoy returned home late from a day with the Chertkovs, she lay on her bed and screamed at him, "You have no pity, you have a heart of stone, you love nobody but Chertkov, I shall kill myself, you shall see. I shall take poison."[10] It took him hours to calm her.

After the death of Vanichka, Sonya's world became one of moving in and out of rational states. Her anxious concern and obsessive tending to Tolstoy's every need was suffocating and, at times, pitiable. Yet she knew what she wanted. Or perhaps she knew what she did not want. She did not want to give way to Chertkov.

The issue between them—that is, the surface one—was that of the copyrights to her husband's writing, and it was complicated. By a diary entry of 1885, Tolstoy had made his wishes known clearly: Sonya was to hold the copyright to all works published before 1881, and presumably the resources from those most successful novels would be distributed to the Tolstoy children upon her death. Thus their inheritance was tied to this diary entry. As to the writings after the spiritual conversion—that is, after 1881—it was Tolstoy's wish that they be in the public domain. These works were published for the most part by The Intermediary, the press which Chertkov directed. The Intermediary served as the editorial base for the later Tolstoy works, including, so it was revealed, his diaries from 1900 on.

In June of 1909, Sonya begged her husband for reassurance, by way of a signed document, that her copyright, not legally protected by a diary entry, was secure. Tolstoy refused to discuss it. Swirling around her was a conspiratorial atmosphere worthy of a light opera, if the implications had not been so serious: The Leo Tolstoy partisans—Alexandra, her friend Varvara Mikhailovna, Chertkov, Goldenweiser, and a Chertkov aide named Strakhov—gathered behind closed doors with the Master in the Remington room. From outside the door Sonya could hear their voices, hear her name mentioned, hear derision. At teatime, they either ignored her or were obsequiously polite. Tolstoy seemed to be nice to her "on principle" (her words) instead of out of genuine kindness. Her powers of observation were not always clouded by her emotional excesses.

At Chertkov's request, Alexandra had taken it upon herself to record for him the daily difficulties that her father suffered at the hand of his distraught wife, a job from which she did not shrink. And, sadly, Sonya provided any number of incidents from which they could draw inference. She once ran out into the rain and lay down in a ditch, demanding that Tolstoy himself come out and bring her in. She screamed, threatened to drown herself, and at times neither ate nor slept. In her diary she refers to Tolstoy's "heartless and cruel attitude" toward her. June 16, 1910: "Another tormenting day. It is four o'clock in the morning and I have not been to bed . . . I feel very ill. Is it possible that I shall not die? Lev Nikolayevich is still angry and indifferent as before. I torment him, he is to be pitied. But he has health and mental strength while I am perishing."[11]

But she wasn't perishing, and there was more to come to test her strength. Tolstoy had given Chertkov his later diaries, the ones from 1900 onward. Therein lay the record of his discord with his wife. Sonya cared very much about her place in history, how she would be perceived, and she knew that Chertkov would use these documents to discredit her. "I saw her run into father's room," Alexandra tells us in her book *The Tragedy of Tolstoy*.

> "Ah!" my mother screamed. "Ah! Chertkov has stolen them, has taken them away by trickery. Where are they, where?"
> "I don't know, Sonya, this is really not important."
> "It's not important to me, but it is important to Chertkov, isn't it? Why is it less important to me, your wife, than to this devil Chertkov?"
> "Because he has devoted his whole life to me, he is occupied with my works, because he is the nearest person of all." And father started to leave the room.
> "Kill me! Give me Opium!" Mother screamed.[12]

Of the many quoted exchanges between these two elderly warriors, this is one of the cruelest, for in the simple phrase "he is the nearest person of all" were echoed Sonya's worst fears. Chertkov had taken her rightful place. And why had Tolstoy given the diaries up? Chertkov had convinced him of their historical importance, the need to use these most private documents as a "reference."

The Tolstoy diaries are of significance, although they are replete with countless references to his gastrointestinal problems, which may or may not have historical importance. The private documents of all great men are interesting. Yet they were also considered sacred; by giving these pages to "the one who has divided us," Tolstoy seemed to give up anything that was left of his private married world. Though her reaction ("Give me Opium") was wild and melodramatic, the provocation was there and was hard to miss. Sonya, now anxious to the point of dementia, threw her entire being into getting the diaries back into her house.

What she did not know (but could she sense it?) was that those very diaries contained reference to yet another intrigue which was potentially death-dealing. At Chertkov's prodding, Tolstoy had signed a will making *all*

Tolstoy stands outside Chertkov's rented dacha, near Yasnaya Polyana, in 1907.

of his works public property. This will, though later proved to be unofficial, negated the all-important statement of 1885 guaranteeing Sonya's copyright of his early works. References to this secret act were made in the diary, which she now demanded be returned to her at Yasnaya Polyana. Alexandra plainly states: "Chertkov and I were very much afraid that father would finally consent and give mother the diaries."[13] Indeed.

Alexandra is a perplexing figure. Most biographers chronicle the last months of Tolstoy's life as a pitch battle between Sonya and Chertkov, and yet Alexandra's role in this final struggle is as important as any of the principals. Physically, she was bulky and graceless, and like her parents prone to jealousy. She lacked moderation and was capable of stinging, cruel gestures. (She once spit at her mother.) Yet, she was very intelligent, resourceful, and perhaps the most interesting of the Tolstoy daughters. The problem was that she had, years earlier, lost the regard for her mother that might give her any sense of balance in the war between her parents. Her devotion to her father, her passion for him, at times very touching, nonetheless made her the natural ally of Chertkov. And it was she who tipped the balance.

On July 14, 1910, a weary and tormented Tolstoy sent her to Telyatinki to pick up the diaries. Chertkov, meanwhile, had had his staff copy on separate sheets all references damaging to Sonya—feverishly recording these passages lest they be lost to history—then, solemnly making the sign of the cross over the beleaguered documents, sent them back to Yasnaya with Alexandra. For Sonya's eyes? No, she was not to read them, for a promise had been struck; at Tolstoy's instruction the diaries were to be locked in the bank at Tula. When Alexandra arrived back at Yasnaya Polyana, Sonya apparently flung herself on the diaries with vehemence and had to be pried loose. Although she held them, she did not read them. But she felt their contents and was not at rest.

Earlier in that fateful year, a young student named Valentin Bulgakov had been brought in by Chertkov to be Tolstoy's secretary. Bulgakov kept a record of those last months at Yasnaya Polyana which has become invaluable, because he managed, despite or perhaps because of his profound devotion to Leo Tolstoy, to be objective. He tried to intercede on Sonya's behalf in the matter of the diaries; he understood her anguish. Though he was sympathetic to Tolstoy and loved him deeply, the young secretary was not blind to his faults. So that when on July 22 Bulgakov describes Sonya as being "in a dreadful state," we believe him.

"Nervous and upset, she was rude and antagonistic, not alone to the guests but to everyone present. The effect this created was understandable; everyone was strained and dejected. Chertkov looked as if he had swallowed a poker; he drew himself up and his face turned to stone. The samovar boiled cheerily on the table, the bowl of raspberries stood out like a bright red patch on the white tablecloth, but those sitting around the table looked as though they were serving a prison sentence and hardly touched their tea. No one stayed very long."[14] Some tea party.

We learn from Bulgakov that a psychiatrist, G. I. Rossolimo, had been sent for from Moscow to examine the distraught Countess Tolstoy. He was accompanied by a Tolstoy faithful, Dr. Nikitin, and together they decided that Sonya was suffering from extreme paranoia and hysterics. No reasonable remedies were offered—there were none. But they agreed that she was not insane.

In the afternoon of July 22 (the same day that Bulgakov described Sonya as nervous and antagonistic), another strangely fanciful scene had taken place. In the woods, some few short versts from his house, Tolstoy, sitting on a tree stump, rewrote his will. His lawyer, an incompetent named Maraviov, had discovered the will that Tolstoy signed earlier to be invalid. For days Tolstoy had suffered renewed doubts about the entire business—the secrecy, the constant changes, the pressure from Chertkov, his obligations to his followers.

Chertkov took the position that, having renounced all property ownership, Tolstoy, at his death, needed to continue that example by leaving everything he wrote in the public domain. This view won out. Finally—to avoid Sonya—Tolstoy, Goldenweiser, and a few advisers took to the woods.

This will left all copyrights to Alexandra, with the clear understanding that, as executor, she would carry out her father's wishes. In addition, another statement was prepared guaranteeing that Tolstoy's writings were to become public property and that all manuscripts were to be *kept and edited by Chertkov*. Thus Chertkov would assume control of the works of Leo Tolstoy. It also meant, this small, innocent sentence, that a publisher could run off and sell copies, not only of the later moral writings but of *Anna Karenina* and *War and Peace*. Sonya, and presumably her heirs, would no longer be able to ask for copyright fees.

Alexandra's tone in telling of the will-signing in the forest is distant at best. "I know how difficult it was for father to come to this decision and what a trial it was to be unable to tell the family what he had done."[15] But could she have missed the irony of the moment? Tolstoy, the prophet of truth and brotherly love, the conscience of the nineteenth century, the author of *War and Peace,* huddled in the forest with Chertkov's secretary and other little gnomes as witnesses, signing a secret will. She adds, stoutly, "But he had firmly decided to wipe out, if only after his death, the compromises which he had tolerated during his lifetime."

On the twenty-sixth, though Sonya seemed to be losing more control by the day, her sixth sense was still alert. She notes, "There is certainly some secret plot between Lev Nikolayevich and Chertkov against me and the children." It must be noted that the "plot," as it stood at that point, would not have left her destitute (that is, unless one could anticipate the 1917 revolution). But the struggle was always about more than legalities. Sonya, further distraught, sat down and composed an irrational letter of farewell to her husband. On July 30 Tolstoy wrote in his new, secret diary: "Chertkov has drawn me into strife, and that strife is very hard and repulsive to me."[16]

But it was his biographer Pavel Birukoff who set in motion further anguish. While visiting Yasnaya Polyana a few days later, Birukoff pointed out something that the others seemed to have missed—that the secrecy of the will ran against all of Tolstoy's convictions. Despite the risk of a huge and possibly destructive reaction from Sonya, Birukoff pleaded that Tolstoy call his family together and reveal, simply and honestly, his intentions and the contents of the will. The plea was in vain. More letters. More sleepless nights. More secrecy.

On August 2, Tolstoy wrote: "I've realized my mistake very, very clearly. I should have summoned all my heirs and announced my intentions, and not kept it secret. I've written all this to Chertkov. He was very upset. She [Sonya] rummages about in my papers." The next day, August 3: "I go to bed with anguish in my heart, and wake up with the same anguish. I just can't overcome it . . . A letter from Chertkov. He's very upset.* . . . In the evening an insane note from Sofya Andreyevna and a demand that I read it. I glanced at it and gave it back. She came in and began to talk. I locked myself in, then ran away and sent Dushan [Dr. Makovitsky] to her. How will this end?"[17]

How was it to end? How could it end except in some extraordinary way? Such were the properties of the life of Leo Tolstoy.

At the time of the publication of *War and Peace,* Tolstoy said: "It is a terrible thing when characters in a story do what is not in their nature to do." Here before us stood Tolstoy, now eighty-two, a figure who personified the diverse aspects of man's nature: the man who preached chastity while fathering thirteen children, the landowner who renounced property but still lived in reasonable comfort on his own estate. How could it all end, this complicated, contradictory life?

It would be reasonable, would it not, to hope that a man of Tolstoy's stature and advanced age, his work done, might die peacefully in his own bed. But such was not his nature.

Too many questions remained unresolved. One of the great forces of his life—his estate, Yasnaya Polyana—now seemed an unendurable burden, both of conscience and circumstance. For years he had been plagued with guilt about the property. All of the gestures designed to distance himself from the ownership of Yasnaya had not masked the fact that he was still there. Still in

---

* Chertkov defended the secrecy of the will on the grounds that he suspected that, after Tolstoy's death, Sonya and her sons would sue to gain *all* copyrights of his works.

nuance of his health were constant; such attention is enough to kill a man.

And among family and staff, another preoccupation: Sensing that the end of this most spectacular life was at hand, anyone who could hold a pen was gathering notes for his own version of The Final Days of Leo Tolstoy. Bookshelves in libraries now sag with these many references, some more valuable than others. In fact, so much has been written about Tolstoy's death that it sometimes threatens to unbalance the full picture of his life.

Day by day, the fortress mentality at Yasnaya brought sad disillusion. Each of its residents walked an emotional tightrope. Confrontations, night wanderings, threats and shouting—this all within the walls of the home of the foremost advocate of brotherly love. In September a huge scene ensued over the hanging of a photograph in Tolstoy's study; later Alexandra stormed out of the house, to move (briefly) to Telyatinki. Sonya made accusations of homosexual leanings between Tolstoy and Chertkov. Through this, a new (and equally secret) will had to be signed, because those in the forest had forgotten to dictate an essential phrase. At one point, in late September, Sonya lost her head so completely that she wandered about the house firing a toy pistol into the air. Where were the "gentle caresses of the old house"?

Yasnaya Polyana, where once Tolstoy had felt the more perfect comfort—that is, the comfort of the spirit—now only tormented him. Oh, to be away from Yasnaya—to be rid of estate life! During these last months, the place which had harbored his most creative and idyllic thoughts had become a scene of near trench warfare. Love was to unite the world, was it not? And now, here in his own house, animosity ruled the day. "I was in error," he confessed, "that love does its own work."[20]

A weary Tolstoy continued to cling to Alexandra. He only wanted peace, and of course she could provide little of that. But she protected him. He resisted any temptation to turn away from Chertkov and the partisans at Telyatinki. As for Sonya, so vulnerable and outrageous, he tried to hold himself above her excesses; his aloofness only served to make her more desperate. Toward the end of August he confided in his diary: "She is completely hopeless, her thinking is so inconsistent. She is terribly pitiable and difficult. Something is going to happen. Help me, God, to be with Thee and to do Thy will."

On August 29, from Tanya's estate at Kochety, he wrote Sonya a letter which, by his own description, flowed from the heart:

You touched me deeply, dear Sonya, by your good and sincere words on leaving. How good it would be if you could conquer in yourself that—I don't know how to say it—that which tortures you. How good it would be for you and for me. I do not stop thinking about you. I am writing what I feel and I do not want to write anything superfluous. Please write.

Your loving husband,
L.T.[21]

This is surely proof, and proof *was* needed, of the bond between them and of his ability to be, at least in writing, devoted and kind. But Sonya, so

Last photo of Tolstoy and Sonya together.

deeply entrenched in her damaged emotions and confusion, answered him with fleeting tenderness but almost incoherently. The day after receiving Tolstoy's ingratiating letter, she sent for a priest whom she directed to sprinkle holy water in all the rooms where Chertkov had sat, that she might "smoke him out," with incense. Thus she continued on her dangerous path.

Tolstoy by this time had become something of a figure in the image of Job—upright, beleaguered, his faith tested by misfortune. He wrote on September 24: "A letter from Chertkov with reproaches and accusations. They are tearing me to pieces." The next day: "All of my business is with God and I must be alone."[22] On October 3, Tolstoy suffered a brief series of convulsions which left him unconscious and twitching uncontrollably. Bulgakov sat in attendance with the others through the night, with visions of "that pale, ghastly, harrowed face, with its knit brows and indomitable expression." The next morning he was better. Bulgakov records: "The danger has passed."

Days later, a seven-year-old granddaughter, Vera (Ilya's daughter), visited Yasnaya with her parents. As they got on the train to go home, the child burst into tears, tears "for Grandmother and Grandfather," whose tragedy she did not understand but could feel in every part of her being.

October 27, Sonya noted in her diary that it had snowed. That night, at three in the morning, almost reflexively following her instincts, she made her way to Tolstoy's study as he slept nearby and started searching through his desk drawer. Tolstoy awoke with a start. He lit his candle. They spoke briefly, then she went back to her room. This night visitation, the sight of her rummaging through his desk, left him so indignant and in a state of such anxiety that he thought he might have a heart attack.

He lay still but found himself flooded with resolve. Apparently there is such a thing as the last straw. He waited until four, then dressed quickly, wrote his wife a letter of farewell, woke Alexandra, then Dr. Makovitsky, told them that he was leaving. Trembling, he bid them to make preparations. What had been a dream of escape was now formed and in earnest.

Alexandra stuffed his necessities in a bag. Makovitsky, who was to accompany him, packed medicines and blankets. Tolstoy went out into the night to rouse the stable hands and get them to ready the carriage. In the pitiless darkness, he lost his way, unusual for him, and his hat blew off; he had to return to the house to get a lantern. He was terrified lest any of them, in the fever of preparation, might wake Sonya. At the stables he struggled to help the coachmen with the horses, while Alexandra, her companion Varvara, and Makovitsky made their way through trees and the mud paths with the baggage. The nightmare of the departure overshadowed the question—Where were they to go?

Though weakened by his recent illness, Tolstoy did think relatively clearly. They would leave Alexandra at Yasnaya to cope with Sonya; Makovitsky and he would take a train from Yasenki station, avoiding Tula, and head south for the Shamardino Convent. There his sister, Marya, the last of his family from his own generation, lived in peaceful solitude as a nun. Peaceful solitude, at this desperate point, was the only thing he could hope for. Her convent lay some ten short miles from the Optina Monastery, where they knew him and would take him in. One can only note with passing irony that the moment of crisis found him turning to the monks of the Orthodox church, whose rituals he had so vigorously opposed. But nothing mattered—only escape.

Their train was filled with tobacco smoke; they rode in second, and then third class, everyone recognized him, spoke to him, it was icy cold, and he was deeply tired. It is not clear if, at this point, he allowed himself to feel the magnitude of what he had done.

Sonya, his wife of forty-eight years—*left behind*. Yasnaya Polyana, where he had mowed the fields, planted his orchard—*left behind*. The contradictions built into his life there, the struggle between his disciples and his family—*left behind*. He wrote in his diary, "It seems to me that I have saved myself—not Lev Nikolayevich, but that something of which there is sometimes a spark in me."[23] A spark in him! A spark remained, brought to life, as he rode away from his estate for the last time. Despite the fact that he was surely as much at fault as anyone for the mess at Yasnaya Polyana, the vivid sense of suffocation that surrounded him during the last weeks at home causes the observer to bid him free himself, go, and Godspeed.

So he had torn away in the middle of a winter's night in an open carriage, a droshky. The Russian spirit has always been steeped in dramatized knowledge—to live what one knows as actors on a stage—and now at last, after all the years of talk, he had left manorial life, he had staged a huge retreat. Little did he suspect that within forty-eight hours, all the world would be his audience.

*   *   *

They spent the night at the Optina Hostelry. Exhausted, perhaps exhilarated, surely apprehensive. Before he slept, Tolstoy sent telegrams to Chertkov and Alexandra, announcing his safe arrival, but carefully, he made no mention of where he was. The next morning Tolstoy walked in the monastery gardens, talked to the brothers, and after a lunch of simple cabbage soup, got back in the droshky and made the nine-mile trip to his sister's convent, Shamardino.

At Yasnaya Polyana, Sonya did not waken until eleven in the morning; Bulgakov and Alexandra were waiting for her with Tolstoy's letter. Alexandra's account:

> "Where is papa?" she asked in a frightened voice.
> "Father has gone!"
> "Where?"
> "I don't know."
> She seized the letter and read quickly. "He has left! Left for good!" mother screamed. "Farewell, I cannot live without him any longer. I shall drown myself!"[24]

She ran out of the house, down the lane toward the pond. Servants rushed in, alarmed. Bulgakov followed her from one direction, Alexandra from the other. At the jetty by the pond, she stopped, looked back, then jumped in. At this point, Semyon the cook, Vanya the footman, Bulgakov and Alexandra rushed into the water, gently pulled her out, and carried her back to the house.

She regained some presence of mind, briefly, and dispatched a telegram to Tolstoy at the station ordering his return and signed it with Alexandra's name. (He was long gone by this time.) Forced by her housekeeper to change her sodden clothes, she became hysterical again, demanded opium, and continually beat her breast with a penknife. An hour later she headed back toward the pond, where the same team ran off to retrieve her. Alexandra sent for Tanya, Sergei, Andrei, Misha, and Ilya—and, mercifully, a psychiatrist from Tula. They all assumed hourly watches by her bedside.

The next day, Sonya, alternately weeping, then condemning her husband, roamed the house clutching a tiny pillow she had made for him. The Tolstoy children, all gathered at the point of crisis, held tense, inconclusive discussions. They wrote to their father; Sonya, too, wrote an impassioned plea for his return. Misha played a round of vigorous waltzes on the piano, for no known reason. The day was further complicated by the arrival of a family friend, Prince Obolensky, who took it upon himself to inform the newspapers about the departure of Tolstoy from Yasnaya Polyana. At midnight on October 29, Alexandra and Varvara, bearing the letters and other necessities, hired two carriages and drove through the night to Shamardino. Alexandra had succeeded in keeping Tolstoy's plans secret. No one else in the family knew where he was.

Tolstoy embraced his sister. Steady, solid, Marya Nikolayevna, now a nun, forever his own blood, was in sympathy with him, as he suspected she would be. Divided by their religious beliefs, they were still united by history. Should Sonya follow him to Shamardino, Marya announced that she would deal with her. Marya knew Sonya well; she was fond of her.

For a few hours, Tolstoy felt some repose, so much so that he considered staying near his sister, near the monastery. In fact, he did find a little *izba,* a peasant hut which he intended to rent, to settle in and lead the Spartan but pure life which had so eluded him. Alexandra's arrival disrupted that plan.

She brought news of Sonya, which he eagerly awaited, and the many letters, but she also seemed to bring with her her own brand of urgency. They must go on, she demanded. What if he should be discovered here and be forced to return to Yasnaya?

With a map open in front of them, Makovitsky, Alexandra, Varvara, and Tolstoy, uncertain and in haste, made a loose plan: Either they would go to a cousin in Novocherkassk or perhaps they would go to Bulgaria or the Caucasus. But they would keep moving. Of Tolstoy's state of mind at this point, Alexandra tells us:

> Father only sighed heavily several times, and to my inquiring glance said, "My mind is heavy." I felt grieved as I looked at him. He was so sad and upset. He spoke little and went to bed early.
>
> About four o'clock in the morning, I heard someone knock at our door. I jumped up and opened it. Before me stood father— just as he had stood a few days before—with a candle in his hand.
>
> "Dress quickly, we are going right away," he said.[25]

And another night departure was set in motion.

A word about Dr. Makovitsky: He deeply loved Tolstoy, perhaps to the point where he became more of a partisan than a doctor. It is clear at this point that Leo Tolstoy was more than heavy at heart. At age eighty-two he was frail, he had recently been sick, and his face bore a transparency, a suggestion of death. Makovitsky offered no resistance to these ludicrous travel plans, he could offer no restraint to Alexandra's urgency. He took a fine pulse, but he was no one's idea of a great doctor. They plunged onward.

Back on the train at Kozelsk. By this time the passengers had heard of his flight and leaned in at him, with constant questions. Tolstoy asked for some newspapers, where the terrible fact became clear—word of his departure from Yasnaya was writ bold, and in some detail. He asked Alexandra to cover him with a blanket and tried to sleep.

The car in which they were riding was drafty and he asked for more covers. By morning Tolstoy was running a temperature. They made him tea. The fever rose. To Alexandra's alarmed expression he murmured: "Don't lose heart, Sasha, all is well."

She didn't lose heart, but the sense of their true situation did finally sweep through her:

"For the first time, I realized that we had no shelter—no home. A second class carriage filled with tobacco smoke, strange people around us—and not a spot on earth where we could take refuge with a sick, aged man. We passed Dankov and approached some large station. It was Astapovo."[26]

Astapovo. A small town in the middle of Russia. Astapovo—soon to become a household word.

Tolstoy's mind was wandering and his breathing was labored. They could not go on. Makovitsky raced out onto the platform and made a hasty arrangement: Tolstoy would be allowed to leave the train and lie down in the stationmaster's house. Supporting him on each side, surrounded by onlookers, they guided him gently to the little four-room house right by the tracks, where a bed had been hastily prepared.

He spent a restless night, plagued with fever and convulsions, but by the next morning he seemed better. Could they go on? he asked. No, they must wait. He then asked Alexandra to send for Chertkov. Later in the afternoon he dictated letters to Sergei and Tanya, begging them not to come but to stay with Sonya, for he didn't feel he could see her under any circumstances. That night, the night of November 2, his temperature rose again, this time to 102°. He moved in and out of light states of delirium, and Dr. Nikitin was called in from Moscow. At nine in the evening Chertkov arrived; at this point he was genuinely needed, for he was calm and steady and the principals were by this time utterly exhausted. Tolstoy dictated a sentence to Alexandra: "God is the unlimited all, man is only the limited expression of God."[27] As Tolstoy lay on his bed, the stationmaster's three children played merrily in the tiny room next door.

At Yasnaya Polyana, Sonya and her family waited, sensing only that everything that could be wrong had gone wrong but not knowing where he was. Then, as if a gift from heaven, a telegram addressed to Sonya came in from a newspaper correspondent: "Lev Nikolayevich has fallen ill at Astapovo. Temperature 104." Astapovo! Sonya collected herself admirably, hired a special train, and, accompanied by her psychiatrist, a nurse, Tanya and Andrei, Ilya and Misha, and a variety of medicines and pillows, headed for Astapovo.

In the interim, both the Russian and international press had discovered Tolstoy's whereabouts. Suddenly the little red stationmaster's house was surrounded with eager journalists and photographers, some from as far away as News-Pathé in France, all jockeying for position, trying (and later succeeding) to get film of the family pacing around the station. Anyone coming in and out of the house was besieged with questions. County police were called in to keep order. Sundry clergy sought an audience with the dying man. A day later, November 3, amid this mayhem, Sonya's train pulled into the station.

Alexandra, acting in what she believed to be her father's best interests, using Makovitsky as emissary, forbade her mother entrance to the house. Four times Sonya escaped the watch of her nurse and sons and made her way to the door of the house, where she was turned back. She remained for the most part in the railway carriage, "torn to pieces by my conscience, the expectation of a bad ending and the impossibility of seeing my beloved husband."[28] As Goldenweiser, Sergei, and Tanya visited the bedside, Chertkov posted his assistant at the door and allowed no one in without his permission. Sonya began giving interviews to the restless press. In the midst of this, Tolstoy, oblivious to the lurid activity outside his door, asked Dr. Nikitin, "What about the muzhiks? How do the muzhiks die?"

His condition worsened. Dr. Makovitsky wrote, "Lev Nikolaevich slept little. He could not settle down, but groaned, tossed about raised himself high on the bed with wonderful ease, even sat up . . ."[29] Wonderful ease! Even as he lay dying, his strength ebbing, he remained a powerful physical presence.

The snowy streets of Astapovo were now clogged with the world press, many sleeping in railway cars. Each change of temperature or new diagnosis was announced to the waiting journalists, who then communicated these clinical morsels to the world. The Holy Synod, ever alert, dispatched an emissary, Father Varsonofi, to see if he could get a last-minute reconversion from this, the most powerful moral voice of the nineteenth century. Alexandra dealt with Father Varsonofi decisively.

More doctors arrived bearing oxygen and morphine. On the evening of November 5, Tolstoy whispered to his daughter Tanya, "Much has fallen upon Sonya. We have planned badly . . ." Such important words! Although there remains a dispute as to whether he did at this point wish to see her, it is clear, by this simple thought, that he still cared for her and was aware of her burdens. At this point Tolstoy was unsure as to where she was, but he assumed that she was still at Yasnaya Polyana. She remained in her railroad car.

Despite the pneumonia that was raging through his system, Tolstoy had periods of complete clarity. To Chertkov, who read to him at sleepless moments, he said, "It seems I am dying; but perhaps not." As his pulse grew weaker and he had more trouble breathing, the flurry of activity from over-

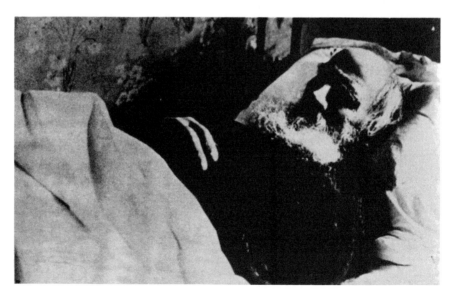

Tolstoy on his deathbed.

wrought doctors irritated him: "What is this treatment for? God will arrange everything." They gave him an injection of camphor. Later he called for Sergei and murmured to him, "Truth . . . I have much love, . . ." and fell back on his pillow.[30]

Finally, at two o'clock in the morning of November 7, Sonya was admitted to his side; he had slipped into unconsciousness. She kissed him on the forehead, then knelt by his bedside murmuring, "Forgive me, forgive me." She continued her lamentations as his face settled into its final mask, at once stern and serene. Everyone was quiet, waiting. At five minutes after six in the morning, in a room by a railroad track, he stopped breathing.

Tolstoy is dead! The word spread like wildfire throughout his Russia and the rest of the world. All newspapers bore his picture framed in black. The Tsar voiced his sympathy. University lectures were canceled, a day of public mourning proclaimed. Those who had opposed him sent messages of genuine respect. Those who had followed him felt massive grief. Those who needed him were frightened.

Mourners carry Tolstoy's body from the stationmaster's house at Astapovo, for the trip home.

This death, this wild death, preceded by his flight, could be interpreted as a kind of renunciation of everything. It surely was seen as a disavowal of estate life, a continuation of his moral evolution. He did not die as a muzhik, alas, as perhaps he had wished to. But neither did he die as a patriarch, safe in his own bed. He died as a restless spirit, wandering, searching, away from home. Did he come closer to God, there in the railroad station? How can we know?

Gorky wrote: "There is a dog howling in my soul, and I have a feeling of foreboding . . . I imagine him in his coffin; he lies like a smooth stone at the bottom of a stream."[31]

As the announcement of Tolstoy's death reached peasants and workers, they gathered at Astapovo station, placing themselves where he was, that they might be near him one more time. Schoolchildren filed by his bier, men made the sign of the cross, women sobbed. Sonya sat quietly by the coffin; though dazed, she carried herself with dignity and restraint.

All over Russia people crowded to news billboards to read of his death, to pass on the news; and the authorities, fearing demonstrations, encouraged a swift departure from Astapovo. This apostle of nonviolence, twenty-four hours after his death, still threatened the existing order. On the morning of

Thousands gather to join the funeral procession through the fields of Yasnaya Polyana to the burial site.

November 8, four of Tolstoy's sons carried his coffin out of the stationmaster's house and onto a waiting train. A freight car had been readied, filled with pine boughs and notes and messages of love from the people. At last the convoy pulled out of the station to return Tolstoy to Yasnaya Polyana, the place from which he had fled some twelve days earlier. The sky was overcast and the air still and cold. At 6:30 the next morning, his train arrived at the small station of Zasyeka, the closest point to the house. A crowd, extraordinary in number—four thousand—had gathered; friends, delegations from Moscow, neighbors, peasants from Yasnaya Polyana, students, and partisans, as well as photographers and government-assigned policemen. A procession seemed to form itself, with two peasants at the very front holding a banner which read, "Dear Lev Nikolayevich, the memory of your goodness will not die among us, the orphaned peasants of Yasnaya Polyana." Again, Sergei, Misha, Andrei, and Ilya carried the coffin through the frozen fields and onto the road, the road where Tolstoy had walked so many times before.

Yasnaya Polyana stood ready to have him back. The earth which he loved would receive him, the birch trees would surround him, as they so often had. The crowd surged toward the grave site—the spot where he and his brothers had played as children. No priest, no cross, no symbols of the church

Sonya at Tolstoy's grave.

were permitted—this is what he would have wanted. Yet they sang the funeral hymn "Eternal Memory." Begun slowly, defiantly, the singing gathered force. Eternal Memory. An old man whom no one knew spoke briefly. Tolstoy's coffin was lowered into the ground, and, at the crowd's insistence, the policemen knelt. Then slowly, silently, they all moved away. It was the largest public burial in the history of Russia.

The ardent spirit of Leo Tolstoy was finally at rest, his towering personality and the vigor of his pen quiet at last. His grave stood but a brief walk from the spot where he was born. Perhaps now, at this short distance, his soul might again feel the flowing of the Voronka River and the gentle caresses of the old house.

EPILOGUE : YASNAYA POLYANA AFTER LEO TOLSTOY

The fate of the Tolstoy family and that of Yasnaya Polyana became even more intimately joined following Leo Tolstoy's death.

After a period of agonizing grieving, Sonya slowly brought herself to face practical matters. The estate was in disarray. Money was in short supply. She asked for and received a pension from Tsar Nicholas II, a traditional bit of royal munificence but nonetheless generous, considering the amount of trouble that Tolstoy had given the monarchy.

Alexandra and Chertkov held tight to the reins as executors of Tolstoy's writings. For two years after his death, not one word of Leo Tolstoy's was published outside Chertkov's own press. In February of 1913, Alexandra sold the copyright to her father's complete works and the license to publish another full edition for a total sum of 400,000 roubles, which allowed her to buy back from her mother most of the land of Yasnaya Polyana. Then, in accordance with Tolstoy's will, Alexandra gave all but the house and two hundred acres to the peasants. Sonya, fulfilling a promise she had made, distributed the 400,000 roubles in equal parts to all of her children and grandchildren.

In the meantime, Sonya had sued Chertkov and Alexandra for the recovery of all of Tolstoy's handwritten manuscripts, which, after a bitter battle, she won back. She then donated all of these invaluable papers to the Rumyantevsky Museum in Moscow.

Tanya Sukhotin-Tolstoy, now a widow herself, moved back to Yasnaya Polyana, along with her enchanting daughter Tanichka. Alexandra paid tentative visits. The Tolstoy sons continued in their loyalty to their mother. Visitors found the Countess Tolstoy to be calm, busy writing her memoirs, bent perhaps on self-vindication but a woman well in control of herself. She prayed at Tolstoy's grave every day.

As the political winds blew toward revolt and anarchy, Yasnaya Polyana, like all manorial estates, was threatened with pillage by an angry peasantry; havoc and destruction in the countryside were an accepted part of life by 1917. When the estate appeared directly threatened by peasants from a nearby town, the villagers of Yasnaya Polyana, the memory of Tolstoy in their hearts, massed at the gate with pitchforks and protected the estate from what surely would have been mass destruction.

For the few remaining residents of Yasnaya Polyana, the revolution of October 1917 knocked everything that was familiar from their lives. They stayed close to the main house, bewildered and afraid, husbanded their few resources, and dreamt of the past. To help raise a few roubles, Tanya knit wool scarves to be sold at the Tula market. In 1918, the property was nationalized and turned into a state farm. Difficult as this was for Sonya, who now was in some sense a guest in her own house, protection was at least somewhat guaranteed.

The assault on Russia from both within and without during this period was extraordinary. In 1914, Russia had entered the First World War, committing huge numbers of troops to battle. In 1917 the tsar and his family were executed, and the Bolsheviks, led by Lenin, took over. A bitter civil war followed between the Communists, the Reds, and the White Russians, a combined force of those who remained loyal to the provisional government of Kerensky and to the monarchy. Throughout this period of constant armed conflict, a great famine swept through the land, killing millions of people.

Cut off from her pension and more or less without income, Sonya, her daughter Tanya, and her sister Tanya Kuminskaya lived on at Yasnaya Polyana, with three loyal old servants and a very bare table. Soldiers were billeted throughout the property, and a red flag flew over the entrance to the main house. At that point perhaps one can only be grateful that Tolstoy was in his grave.

The Tolstoy children, who had held onto their few pieces of property until the Revolution, now faced poverty and possible exile. Alexandra had become disenchanted with Chertkov. Determined and clever, she managed to get herself appointed as the state-appointed manager of Yasnaya Polyana; she returned to find her mother, her past enemy, frail and nearly blind. They embraced, and wept, each begging forgiveness. The old animosity was gone. For days on end, Sonya sat in her armchair and dozed, sustained by memories. The house was underheated and had become shabby. People not known to her wandered through the halls.

In the fall of 1919, while attempting to wash some upstairs windows on a cold day, Sonya caught pneumonia. Death approached quietly but surely. She was attended by her sister and her two daughters, Tanya and Alexandra. Sonya died on November 4, after receiving extreme unction from the church, from whose embrace she had never wandered.

For a few years after her mother's death, Tanya Sukhotin-Tolstoy served as director of the Tolstoy Museum in Moscow. On the grounds of Yasnaya Polyana, Alexandra tried to establish a school which partly reflected her father's ideals, but she ran afoul of the local commissar and the school closed in the late 1920s. Eventually, all the Tolstoy children except Sergei emigrated to Europe and the United States. Russia and Yasnaya Polyana were no longer theirs, and the past could not sustain them.

Today, Yasnaya Polyana, having survived several administrations and World War II, stands beautifully restored. Each room, every desktop and chair, is returned to the exact state it was in on October 28, 1910, the night Leo Tolstoy left the estate in flight.

NOTES

Chapter 1: A Splendid Orphan and the Golden Age of Yasnaya Polyana (1828–1852)

1. Pavel Birukoff, *Leo Tolstoy: His Life and Work* (New York: Charles Scribner's Sons, 1906), 18.
2. Cited in Henri Troyat, *Tolstoy* (New York: Doubleday and Co., 1967), 14.
3. Leo Tolstoy, *Childhood,* Penguin edition (New York: Penguin Books, 1978), 81.
4. Birukoff, *Leo Tolstoy,* 41.
5. Ibid., 8–9.
6. Ibid.
7. Ibid., 54.
8. Ibid.
9. Leo Tolstoy, *Boyhood,* Penguin edition (New York: Penguin Books, 1978), 112.
10. Aylmer Maude, *Life of Tolstoy* (New York: Dodd, Mead and Co., 1910), vol. 1, 28.
11. Birukoff, *Leo Tolstoy,* 48.
12. Ibid., 51.
13. R. F. Christian, ed., *Tolstoy's Diaries* (New York: Charles Scribner's Sons, 1985), 11.
14. Ibid., 14.
15. Maude, *Life of Tolstoy,* vol. 1, 48.
16. Ibid., 50.
17. Birukoff, *Leo Tolstoy,* 110.
18. Christian, *Tolstoy's Diaries,* 11.
19. Ibid., 22.
20. Ibid., 35.
21. Ibid., 33.

Chapter 2: Soldier, Teacher, and a Terrifying Happiness (1852–1862)

1. Cited in Troyat, *Tolstoy,* 93.
2. Christian, *Tolstoy's Diaries,* 103.
3. Maude, *Life of Tolstoy,* vol. 1, 128–130.
4. Christian, *Tolstoy's Diaries,* 100.
5. Birukoff, *Leo Tolstoy,* 193.
6. Maude, *Life of Tolstoy,* vol. 1, 132.
7. Christian, *Tolstoy's Diaries,* 154.
8. Ibid., 118–119.
9. Maude, *Life of Tolstoy,* vol. 1, 179.
10. Nathan Haskell Dole, *Life of Lyof N. Tolstoi* (New York: Thomas Crowell, 1911), 146.
11. Maude, *Life of Tolstoy,* vol. 1, 246.
12. Cited in Troyat, *Tolstoy,* 193.
13. Maude, *Life of Tolstoy,* vol. 1, 232.
14. Ibid., 238.
15. V. S. Morozov, *Reminiscences of Lev Tolstoi by His Contemporaries* (Moscow: Foreign Languages Publishing House, 1960), 148.
16. Cited in Troyat, *Tolstoy,* 220.
17. Maude, *Life of Tolstoy,* vol. 1, 291.
18. Ibid., 57.
19. Morozov, *Reminiscences,* 149.
20. Cited in Troyat, *Tolstoy,* 225.
21. Maude, *Life of Tolstoy,* vol. 1, 287.
22. Ibid., 289.
23. Ibid., 288.
24. Christian, *Tolstoy's Diaries,* 166.
25. Ibid., 168.
26. A. Werth, ed. and trans., *The Diary of Tolstoy's Wife* (New York: Payson and Clarke, 1920), 82.
27. Cynthia Asquith, *Married to Tolstoy* (Boston: Houghton Mifflin Co., 1961), 46.
28. Christian, *Tolstoy's Diaries,* 169.
29. Cited in Boris Eikhenbaum, *Tolstoi in the Sixties* (Ann Arbor, Michigan: Ardis Publishers, 1961), 61.
30. Christian, *Tolstoy's Diaries,* 168.
31. Cited in Eikhenbaum, *Tolstoi in the Sixties,* 61.

Chapter 3: *War and Peace* (1862–1869)

1. Maude, *Life of Tolstoy,* vol. 1, 76.
2. Christian, *Tolstoy's Diaries,* 177.
3. Asquith, *Married to Tolstoy,* 53.
4. A. Werth, ed., *Diaries of Countess Tolstoy* (New York: Payson and Clarke, 1920), 104.
5. Tatyana Kuminskaya, *Tolstoy as I Knew Him* (New York: Macmillan, American Council of Learned Societies, 1948), 144.
6. Ibid., 173.
7. Ibid., 144.
8. R. F. Christian, ed., *Tolstoy's Letters* (New York: Charles Scribner's Sons, 1978), vol. 1, 118.

9. Eikhenbaum, *Tolstoi in the Sixties,* 119.

10. Kuminskaya, *Tolstoy as I Knew Him,* 289.

11. Ibid., 291.

12. Count Ilya Tolstoy, *Reminiscences of Tolstoy* (London: Chapman and Hall, 1914), 100.

13. Christian, *Tolstoy's Letters,* 244.

14. Ibid., 193.

15. Troyat, *Tolstoy,* 300.

16. Dole, *Life of Lyof N. Tolstoi,* 214.

17. Christian, *Tolstoy's Letters,* 199.

18. Cited in Troyat, *Tolstoy,* 300.

19. Maude, *Life of Tolstoy,* vol. 1, 325.

20. Kuminskaya, *Tolstoy as I Knew Him,* 376.

21. Maude, *Life of Tolstoy,* vol. 1, 367.

22. Cited in Louise Smoluchowski, *Lev and Sonya* (New York: Paragon House Publisher, 1988), 92, 88.

23. Maude, *Life of Tolstoy,* vol. 1, 367.

Chapter 4: *Anna Karenina* and *A Confession* (1869–1880)

1. Maude, *Life of Tolstoy,* vol. 1, 348.

2. Ibid., 242.

3. Ibid., 333.

4. Cited in Alexandra Tolstoy, *A Life of My Father* (New York: Harper and Brothers, 1953), 205.

5. Christian, *Tolstoy's Letters,* 261.

6. Leo Tolstoy, *Anna Karenina,* Penguin edition (New York: Penguin Books, 1978), 273.

7. Ibid., 827–829.

8. Ilya Tolstoy, *Reminiscences of Tolstoy,* 32.

9. Cited in Troyat, *Tolstoy,* 351.

10. Christian, *Tolstoy's Letters,* 238.

11. Ibid., 280.

12. Ibid., 295.

13. Cited in Troyat, *Tolstoy,* 370.

14. Ibid.

15. Cited in Edward Garnett, *Tolstoy: His Life and Writings* (London: Constable and Co., 1914), 57.

16. Ilya Tolstoy, *Reminiscences of Tolstoy,* 97.

17. Leo Tolstoy, *A Confession,* in *The Portable Tolstoy,* Penguin edition (New York: Penguin Books), 713.

18. Ilya Tolstoy, *Reminiscences of Tolstoy,* 199.

19. Cited in Alexandra Tolstoy, *A Life of My Father,* 238.

20. Cited in Troyat, *Tolstoy,* 95.

21. Ilya Tolstoy, *Reminiscences of Tolstoy,* 95.

22. Tatyana Tolstoy, *Tolstoy Remembered* (New York: McGraw-Hill Book Co., 1977), 185.

23. Tatyana Sukhotin-Tolstoy, *The Tolstoy Home* (New York: Columbia University Press, 1957), 29.

24. Ilya Tolstoy, *Reminiscences of Tolstoy,* 41.

25. Maude, *Life of Tolstoy,* vol. 2, 13.

Chapter 5: A Soul Divided (1880–1890)

1. Maude, *Life of Tolstoy,* vol. 2, 19.
2. Ibid., 22.
3. Christian, *Tolstoy's Diaries,* vol. 1, 195–197.
4. Werth, *Diary of Tolstoy's Wife,* vol. 1, 164.
5. Ibid., 161.
6. Ibid., 192–197.
7. Maude, *Life of Tolstoy,* vol. 2, 91–92.
8. Ibid., 152.
9. Dole, *Life of Lyof N. Tolstoi,* 296.
10. Werth, *Diary of Tolstoy's Wife,* vol. 1, 200.
11. Christian, *Tolstoy's Diaries,* vol. 1, 208.
12. Ibid., 212.
13. Vladimir Tchertkoff, *Last Days of Tolstoy* (London: William Heinemann, 1922), 99.
14. Christian, *Tolstoy's Diaries,* vol. 1, 218.
15. Sukhotin-Tolstoy, *The Tolstoy Home,* 35.
16. Christian, *Tolstoy's Diaries,* vol. 1, 221.
17. Tchertkoff, *Last Days of Tolstoy,* 102.
18. Christian, *Tolstoy's Letters,* vol. 2, 277.
19. Ibid., 319.
20. Werth, *Diary of Tolstoy's Wife,* vol. 1, 211.
21. Maude, *Life of Tolstoy,* vol. 2, 159.
22. Ibid., 210.
23. Ibid., 218.
24. Dole, *Life of Lyof N. Tolstoi,* 322.
25. Maxim Gorky, *Reminiscences of Leo Nikolayevich Tolstoy* (New York: B. W. Huebsch, 1920), 2.
26. Maude, *Life of Tolstoy,* vol. 2, 179.
27. Cited in Garnett, *Tolstoy,* 65.
28. Maude, *Life of Tolstoy,* vol. 2, 182.
29. W. Lakond, *Diaries of Tchaikovsky* (New York: W. W. Norton and Co., 1945), 247.
30. Leo Tolstoy, *The Kreutzer Sonata,* in *The Portable Tolstoy,* Penguin edition (New York: Penguin Books, 1978), 565–571.
31. A. Werth, ed., *The Countess Tolstoy's Later Diaries* (New York: Payson and Clarke, 1928), vol. 2, 19.
32. Derrick Leon, *Tolstoy: His Life and Work* (London: Routledge, 1944), 247.
33. Werth, *Countess Tolstoy's Later Diaries,* 33.
34. Christian, *Tolstoy's Diaries,* vol. 1, 308.

Chapter 6: A Taste for Public Action (1890–1901)

1. A. Werth, *Diaries of Countess Tolstoy* (New York: Payson and Clarke, 1928), vol. 2, 74.
2. Christian, *Tolstoy's Diaries,* vol. 1, 318.
3. Christian, *Tolstoy's Letters,* vol. 2, 481.
4. Christian, *Tolstoy's Diaries,* vol. 2, 314.
5. Ibid., 320.
6. Ibid., 231.
7. Troyat, *Tolstoy,* 507.
8. Christian, *Tolstoy's Diaries,* 401.
9. Christian, *Tolstoy's Letters,* vol. 2, 517.
10. Christian, *Tolstoy's Diaries,* vol. 2, 402.

11. Christian, *Tolstoy's Letters,* vol. 2, 561.
12. Cited in Leon, *Tolstoy,* 277.
13. Cited in Troyat, *Tolstoy,* 536–537.
14. Christian, *Tolstoy's Diaries,* vol. 2, 444.
15. Ibid., 469.
16. Ibid., 450.
17. Ibid., 462.
18. Correspondence of Wilbur Atwater, 19 September 1897.
19. Dole, *Life of Lyof N. Tolstoi,* 375–376.
20. Cited in Troyat, *Tolstoy,* 564.

Chapter 7: Flight (1901–1910)

1. Alexandra Tolstoy, *A Life of My Father,* 460.
2. Christian, *Tolstoy's Diaries,* vol. 2, 566.
3. Alexandra Tolstoy, *A Life of My Father,* 458.
4. Alexandra Tolstoy, *The Tragedy of Tolstoy* (New Haven: Yale University Press, 1933), 176.
5. Alexandra Tolstoy, *A Life of My Father,* 461.
6. Leon, *Tolstoy,* 313.
7. Ibid., 316.
8. Alexandra Tolstoy, *Tragedy of Tolstoy,* 64.
9. Leon, *Tolstoy,* 322.
10. Alexandra Tolstoy, *Tragedy of Tolstoy,* 210.
11. S. L. Tolstoy, ed., *The Final Struggle* (New York: Oxford University Press, 1936), 108.
12. Alexandra Tolstoy, *Tragedy of Tolstoy,* 212.
13. Ibid., 215.
14. Valentin Bulgakov, *The Last Year of Leo Tolstoy* (New York: Dial Press, 1971), 167.
15. Alexandra Tolstoy, *Tragedy of Tolstoy,* 219.
16. S. L. Tolstoy, *Final Struggle,* 194.
17. Christian, *Tolstoy's Diaries,* vol. 2, 678.
18. Ibid., 681.
19. Maxim Gorky, *Reminiscences of Leo Nikolayevich* (New York: B. W. Huebsch, 1920), 67.
20. E. Lampert, "The Body and the Pressure of Time," in Malcolm Jones, ed., *New Essays on Tolstoy* (Cambridge: Cambridge University Press, 1979), 145.
21. Cited in Smoluchowski, *Lev and Sonya,* 255.
22. Christian, *Tolstoy's Diaries,* 683.
23. S. L. Tolstoy, *Final Struggle,* 347.
24. Alexandra Tolstoy, *Tragedy of Tolstoy,* 254.
25. Ibid., 264.
26. Ibid., 268.
27. Ibid., 271.
28. S. L. Tolstoy, *Final Struggle,* 361.
29. Ibid., 360.
30. Leon, *Tolstoy,* 358.
31. Gorky, *Reminiscences of Leo Nikolayevich,* 51–53.

INDEX

That marvelous smell of the woods after a spring thunder-shower, the odour of birches, violets, mouldy leaves, mushrooms and bird cherry blossoms is so delightful that I cannot sit in my carriage but jump from the running board, run over to the bushes and in spite of getting showered with raindrops, tear off wet branches of bird cherry blossoms, beat my face with them and become drunk with their wonderous smell.

—LEO TOLSTOY